The
Restorer's Handbook
of
Ceramics and Glass

Under the direction of Madeleine Hours, chief curator of the National Museums of France, Master of Research at the National Center for Scientific Research.

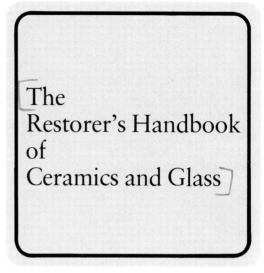

The
Restorer's Handbook
of
Ceramics and Glass

Jean-Michel André

VAN NOSTRAND REINHOLD COMPANY

New York Cincinnati Toronto London Melbourne

To my aunt Denise André

In collaboration with
Denise André
Lucien Stastny
Yves Mérovil
Maurice Michel

English translation: J. A. Underwood

Copyright © 1976 by Office du Livre, Fribourg (Switzerland)

Library of Congress Catalog Card Number: 76-6990

ISBN 0-442-20363-2

Printed in Switzerland

Published in 1976 by Van Nostrand Reinhold Company
A division of Litton Educational Publishing, Inc.
450 West 33rd Street, New York, N. Y. 10001

Van Nostrand Reinhold Limited
1410 Birchmount Road, Scarborough, Ontario M1P 2E7, Canada

16 15 14 13 12 11 10 9 8 7 6 5 4 3 2 1

Library of Congress Cataloging in Publication Data

André, Jean-Michel.

The restorer's handbook of ceramics and glass.

Translation of Restauration de la céramique et du verre.

Bibliography: p. 127

1. Pottery - Repairing.   2. Glassware - Repairing.

I. Title.

NK4233.A5213   738   76-6990

ISBN O-442-20363-2

TABLE OF CONTENTS

INTRODUCTION 7

I   CLEANING 13

Types of fracture 13
Preserving a clean fracture 14
Cleaning a crack 14
Undoing a poor piece of gluing 17
Cleaning fractures on archaeological finds . . 23
Poor fractures 24
Cleaning surfaces 25
Saltpetre rot 26

II   GLUING 27

The jig-saw puzzle 31
Gluing soft earthenware –
archaeological finds 31
    Waterproofing 32
    Gluing 33
    Incomplete finds 37
    Hot-air gluing 38
    Gluing poor fractures 38
    Excess adhesive 40

Gluing glazed earthenware 42
    With polyvinyl adhesive 42
    With epoxy resin 42
Distortion 44
Cyanocrylate adhesives 49
Gluing porcelain 50
Cracked and distorted pieces 50

III   FILLING 53

Filling small holes 53
    Soft earthenware – archaeological finds . . 53
    Filling opaque and glazed wares –
    glazed earthenware and stoneware 56
    Filling with fast-setting epoxy resin 57
    Filling with polyester 57
    Filling to match the glaze colour 57
    Recessed fillings 60
    Filling porcelain 60
Renewing missing fragments 63
    Soft earthenware – archaeological finds . . 63
    Renewing fragments on
    glazed earthenware 66

Renewing fragments on porcelain 71
Renewing missing elements 72
   Soft earthenware – archaeological finds .. 72
   Glazed earthenware and porcelain 76
   Casting 76
   Renewing fragments and elements
   with ceramic ware 77

IV   RETOUCHING 79

Colours 79
Whites 85
Mediums 86
Mat retouching 86
   For museographical purposes 86
   Invisible mat retouching 95
Visible gloss retouching 99
Invisible gloss retouching on
glazed earthenware and porcelain 101
Traditional brush retouching 103
Retouching with a spray gun 106

V   GLASS 109

Gluing modern glass 109
   With cyanocrylates 109
   With epoxy resin 111
   Gluing thick glass 111

Gluing a foot 111
Renewing missing fragments 112
Grinding down 115
Renewing missing elements with
plexiglass 115
Antique glass 115
   Cleaning 115
   Gluing 116
   Renewing missing portions of
   antique glass 117
   Stripe effects 119

CONCLUSION 121

TECHNICAL NOTES 122

Glossary 122
What *not* to do 122
Types of Pottery 123
Equipment 124
Materials 125

BIBLIOGRAPHY 127

Ceramic Techniques 127
Restoration 127

INDEX 128

INTRODUCTION

"Broken crockery and china repaired!"

The cry of the itinerant craftsman has disappeared from the streets of our cities; the Do-It-Yourself counter has supplanted, it seems, the man who used to patch up the crocks of the poor with staples and cement for yet another few years' hard service.

We no longer need him. We throw the bits away and buy a replacement, indifferent to the object as such. The segregation between art and the everyday is nowadays complete.

But if there is no more work for him in the latter domain, in the former his position is as solid as a rock, with employment for years and years to come. The restorer of *objets d'art* is slowly becoming aware of his power over a clientele already resigned to waiting months to save a souvenir, undo the effects of a clumsy moment, or give a rare piece back some commercial value.

Every restorer has his secrets, his own particular "tricks of the trade," his latest discovery. This book, which sets out to survey the ceramic restoration scene, has no intention of giving those secrets away. It proposes to stick to the methods employed by its author – who, though aware that no secret is anything without the hand that executes it, would be only too delighted if his book were to prompt more people to take up the trade. There is more than enough work to go round.

Indeed pottery in all its manifold forms and uses – from the most ordinary saucer to the rarest treasure – is a part of our environment. Born with the invention of fire, ceramics (from χραμ, an ancient Indo-European root that became the Latin *cremo*, "to burn"), the art of fashioning clay and fixing the resultant shape by firing, has continued to hold its own down the centuries, incidentally providing the historian with valuable evidence concerning the evolution of mankind: the soft, unglazed, hand-modelled pottery of the Neolithic age, the first pottery made on the wheel under the early Egyptian dynasties, the first high-quality decoration from Crete, the magnificent flowering of black-figure pottery in sixth-century Attica, the discovery of porcelain in China so many centuries before it was manufactured at Sèvres, the invention of bright-coloured glazes in the Middle East, the development and enrichment of those glazes by Palissy and the Renaissance potters, the technical sophistication of the great eighteenth-century manufacturers. And the Age of Industry, far from neglecting ceramics, has had recourse to it as never before, producing on the one hand a fascinating wealth of art pottery associated with a new art of living and on the other such space-age articles as electronic components and satellite shields.

More than any other art, pottery has its roots in the functional. If sculpture and painting originally had a function it was that of ministering to a god; the first clay pots were fired for the simple purpose of holding food and drink. Gradually, however, as happened with weaving and joinery, pottery became an art: given these everyday utensils, it occurred to man to decorate them, give them an elegant shape, make them lighter and more delicate. The function progressively disappeared until at periods of particular cultural refinement it was no more than a residual pretext. Potters became creators of art objects; there have been great potters as there have been great painters. Possibly there were times when pottery constituted a major art, like cabinet-making in eighteenth-century France: one thinks of the Attic potters of the sixth century B.C.

who signed their works: Ἐξέχιας ἐποίησεν, "Exechias made me." One thinks too of the stoneware used in the Japanese tea ceremony, each piece carefully selected for its meditative potential.

To us, insatiable consumers of the past, inventors of the museum and the flea market, even an amphora – a mere wine bottle – has become an art object, not to mention the whole fantastic output of objects designed to be both useful and beautiful. The craft of the pottery restorer emerged in answer to this demand.

The craft of pottery restoration is as old as every other kind of art restoration – in other words very young indeed.

Leaving aside certain restorations made in classical times with the aid of clumsy lead staples for the sole purpose of getting more use out of some everyday or ritual utensil, and leaving aside the gold-lacquer restorations practised by the Japanese with a view to sublimating an accident (and in this respect coming very close to our modern approach), leaving aside finally twelfth-century Chinese bronze-flux assemblies intended to make the best of a broken celadon, we can say without much fear of contradiction that the restoration of works of art, and of pottery in particular, is an invention of our own day. To be more precise, it is an invention of the nineteenth century, the century of the great archaeological finds and of the great collections of the art of the past put together by Rothschild, Spitzer, Wallace, and others. It was also the first century to reject its own furniture. (Even today there is no question, above a certain level of wealth, of living in any other decor than that of the eighteenth century.)

It was the century of Prosper Mérimée who, as Inspector General of Historical Monuments, drew up an inventory of France's architectural heritage. And it was in the nineteenth century that people began to spend more on the art of the past than they spent on that of the present.

In the circumstances art restoration inevitably went from strength to strength – testifying, perhaps, to a certain impotence on the creative front. (No one in the Middle Ages restored a Romanesque cathedral; they built a bigger Gothic one in its place!) This systematic restoration and conservation of Europe's artistic patrimony justified Hegel's division of the history of art into two periods: a period – now past – of artistic creation and the contemporary period of reflections upon art.

The art object has become a commercial commodity. This is not our doing; beauty has always been sold. Nowadays, however, the price of an art object will depend not only on its beauty but also on its rarity (a not unfair comparison would be stamp-collecting), nor is it hard to see that, in the case of pottery, condition will be a further important factor.

To be valuable a piece must be rare without being too rare. If it is so exceptional that nothing like it ever appears in the salerooms, it will have no quotation and therefore its value will very likely bear no relation to its quality. Greek pottery, for example, is practically all broken, and the few pieces left intact are not necessarily the most beautiful. So whether a piece of Greek pottery is intact or not makes no great difference to its price. The restoration need not be invisible, since deception will serve no purpose, but it will have to be of consummate elegance in order to preserve the integrity of what is left of the original. On the other hand types that generally come up for sale in good condition – Rhodes wares, for example – will have an accepted value, and the price paid will precisely reflect the degree of damage. A mere crack that in no way impairs the beauty of the piece will cut its value by half; a fracture will cut it by three-quarters. The restorer will have no choice but to attempt a restoration that will be invisible to the naked eye, making the piece decorative and saleable again; he cannot hope to give it back its original value. Still, some saleroom buyers find it a good idea to have a pin on them: drawn discreetly across the surface of the glaze, it will distinguish between new and old.

The most dramatic drops in value occur in Chinese pottery and French porcelain. A broken Sung bowl will be worth a twentieth of its value intact. Again there is an element of "stamp-collecting" here, but there is also the undeniable fact that a piece of pottery as delicate and refined as Sung ware has to be intact to be itself. Chinese and in particular Sung ceramic art appeals to more than one of the senses; such wares were designed to be looked at, to be touched, and even to be heard – and of course a broken piece will no longer ring. There would be a great commercial future in invisible restoration if it were not for ultra-violet rays!

Certain pieces escape this drastic law. Suppose for example that a Sung vase with a chip or a crack has been properly repaired; it belongs to a well-known "family" whose members turn up in the salerooms from time to time, but it is of outstanding quality and only a few famous vases tied up in major collections or museums can bear comparison with it. Even damaged and restored, the piece is unique, will stay unique, and will fetch an astronomical price. In the normal course of events, however, restoration, unless it aims to deceive, can only recover part of the value of a piece – and to do even that it must be technically perfect.

There are various methods of restoration available. One possibility is to aim for a totally invisible repair, employing all one's technical skill to copy a milky glaze hinting at hidden depths and to try and find coloured pigments that do not react to ultra-violet light; alternatively one can opt for a simple restoration that makes no attempt to disguise the restored portions. The choice will depend on the piece in question, on the purpose of the restoration, and on the extent of what is technically possible. Some pieces quite obviously ask for an invisible repair; others will not offend if the cracks and restored portions are left in evidence. Why is this? Apart from the fact that archaeological finds are virtually always broken and that we have grown so used to their being broken as almost to prefer them that way, we have to admit to the most profound ignorance – for all the hypotheses of the archaeologists – of the place those finds once occupied in the surroundings and in the lives of those who used them. Perhaps that is the real reason why we so readily accept them for what they are – historical evidence – rather than try to patch them up and fill in the missing bits.

On the other hand we are the grandchildren (comparatively speaking) of the men of the Renaissance and of the eighteenth century and heirs to their possessions; we are perfectly familiar with the setting in which those possessions belonged. A broken artefact of our post-Renaissance civilization is no longer a moving witness to a vanished age; it is a piece of wreckage that only an invisible repair can salvage.

It may seem surprising that a piece of twelfth-century Chinese ware (that far back in time!) also calls for faultless and invisible repair if it is to recover its charm. Apart from the problem of its multi-sensory appeal, however, remember that the sultans of Turkey started buying celadons as early as the fifteenth century and that Chinese wares continued to be imported by the West and copied assiduously until we discovered porcelain ourselves. A Ming porcelain is not all that far removed in spirit from a French faience, despite its three or four-century lead.

Secondly, the destination of the piece to be repaired will also influence the choice between visible and invisible methods. In a museum, for example, things become invested with a certain didactic value and one cannot take the risk of making a false restoration. Museum restorers invent nothing, complete no shape they are not absolutely sure of — some of them going to the extreme of making their repairs so obvious as to be positively distracting.

Even in a museum, however, if the piece has no documentary value in itself but for example forms part of a reconstruction of an interior it can legitimately be repaired in a way that, without striving for the degree of invisibility demanded by the saleroom, will at least be undetectable from a distance. As to what is technically possible, this may well turn out to be the ultimate criterion of whether an invisible or a museographical repair is attempted.

While it is true that a visibly repaired Greek vase does not offend, it is no less true that its metallic black surface is impossible to imitate to perfection. A Hispano-Moorish dish with its coppery highlights may cry out to be made intact: it will be impossible to disguise the fractures except by repainting the whole surface — and sacrificing those inimitable highlights. In both cases the restorer will do better to confine his attentions strictly to the filled or renewed portions, leaving his work slightly visible, perhaps, but at least not spoiling the freshness of the original remainder.

Finally, repairs that may be possible for a genius of restoration may be well beyond a restorer of only average abilities, and the latter will always be wise to content himself with a good, clean, visible repair rather than risk a bad bungle.

The restorer is not interested in the scientific classification of ceramic materials (see the Appendix for Brongniart's system); he has his own way of cataloguing the wares he restores. He is not worried about the chemical composition of earthenware and porcelain; much more important as far as he is concerned are the opacity of the one and the transparency of the other. His classification will range from the most opaque to the most transparent, from the easiest to repair to the most difficult — with glass intruding at the latter extreme as the most transparent material of all and one that is absolutely impossible to repair invisibly. It may also range from the softest to the hardest, from the thickest to the thinnest, from the coldest to the hottest fired — all of which factors will affect the techniques of cleaning, gluing, filling, and retouching with which this book is concerned.

I CLEANING

Pottery restoration is like any other construction or reconstruction operation: you do not "build your house on the sand," and you do not skimp any stage of the process, all of them being equally essential. Gluing sometimes involves feats of acrobatics; retouching calls for a degree of skill that might almost be called a state of grace; cleaning merely requires meticulous care and infinite patience.

Nothing is more important than that the break should be clean; it is no good starting to glue unless all trace of old adhesive, chalk deposit, or dirt has been removed. So the first thing the restorer does is to recreate as far as possible the fresh, clean fractures of a piece of pottery that has just this minute broken.

Types of Fracture

How does a piece of pottery break?
In an enormous variety of ways, of course; still, it is possible to make certain useful distinctions.

The number and shape of the fragments will depend on the quality of the ware concerned, the force of impact, the position of the point of impact, and the shape of the piece.

A flat object such as a plate, if it falls flat on the floor, will often break into two or three large fragments with, if you are lucky, no chipping at all, whereas the same plate subjected to a localized blow may well, while still forming a small number of sizeable fragments, disintegrate into a large number of tiny chips around the point of impact. These chips are usually difficult to recover completely.

A spherical object such as a vase with a narrow neck will inevitably be subjected to a localized blow when falling on the floor. It will take a harder blow than a flat object, its rounded form giving it greater resistance, but beyond a certain degree of force it will smash outwards from the point of impact, that is to say into fragments getting larger the further they are from that point.

A piece of porcelain may break without chipping, being perfectly homogenous in substance. A piece of glazed earthenware, on the other hand, as it separates into fragments, will be subjected to enormous stresses between the glaze, which is extremely hard, and the softer body, resulting in extensive chipping of the glaze along the fractures. Certain localized blows on the edges of a piece may, no matter what type of pottery it is, give rise to fractures or chipping at an angle to the surface of the object. The minute splintering that occurs along the edges of such oblique fractures is particularly problematical.

The best type of fracture is a recent one, at right angles to the surface of the piece, and grainy in texture, which will help the fragments knit together in exactly the right position.

Preserving a clean fracture

You have just dropped a pottery vase.

The first thing to remember is not to impair the fractured edges. This means forgoing the temptation to try over and over again to fit the fragments back together in what you imagine to be an attempt to prove they are all there but is in fact a way of feverishly occupying hands that have started to tremble with shock.

Obviously all the pieces are there – where else could they be? Just be careful to pick them all up, even the tiniest ones, and if you cannot wait until you have calmed down first, at least remember the golden rule: wrap each fragment separately in fluffless tissue paper – or ordinary newspaper will do. Too often the restorer receives a harassed customer who thrusts at him the fragments of the precious victim jingling about in a downy bed of cotton wool. The

once sharp fractures have worn and chipped one another and retouching will be necessary where a good gluing job would have sufficed. Moreover cotton wool is hard to remove completely when cleaning and may get in the way of gluing.

Ideally your vase will have such perfect fractured edges that it can be provisionally reassembled without a drop of glue, holding together by the knit of the grain alone and with the aid of adhesive paper.

Cleaning a crack

Often a piece of hard-paste pottery, glazed earthenware, or porcelain will only be cracked: a hair-line crack begins at one edge and stops in the middle of the piece without forming an actual break. The owner has never felt the need to have the piece retouched; the damage is almost invisible and he has preferred to put up with it. Over the years, however, the crack has filled with dirt until it is now no longer quite so invisible. It needs to be cleaned. Too fine to admit a brush, it will have to spend a few days in a solution of potassium chloride, which will bleach it back to virtual invisibility. If the dirt still shows, a well-fired piece of pottery can safely be boiled in a good detergent. Not many cracks will resist this treatment.

A related problem to cleaning cracks and one that crops up fairly frequently is that of the soft glazed earthenware vessel that has been used to hold fatty

1
Korean bottle. A delicate piece of restoration in gold lacquer. Musée Guimet, Paris.

14

liquids; grease has filtered through the craquelure of the internal glaze and become trapped in the clay beneath it. Here it will be necessary to boil the piece in detergent for quite some time, and even then the treatment may not be completely successful. One can only hope that boiling will get at least some of the discolouring grease out of the clay and so restore something of the original freshness of the glaze and decoration.

Undoing a poor piece of gluing

Usually the immediate consequences of an accident to a piece of pottery are almost as disastrous as the accident itself. Two times out of three the piece that the restorer is presented with has first been subjected to an experimental repair job designed to conceal the damage and so avoid the reproaches customarily administered on such occasions (ills. 3 and 4). But since the unfortunate culprit used the wrong adhesive and his hands were still trembly from the accident, the job was a failure, the last piece stubbornly refused to fit, and so over to the restorer with a "Can you mend it soon, please?" Or more specifically, "Can you mend it before my husband comes back?" Of course the fateful day arrives and the restorer, unreliable fellow that he is, has not got it finished. The ogre returns, the crime is confessed, and a generous pardon shows that the heirloom in question was not after all so close to his

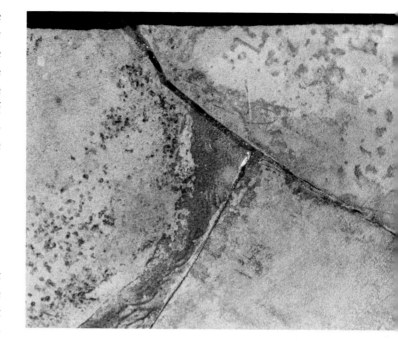

3
A very poor piece of gluing. A great deal of adhesive has been used and the fragments do not meet.

heart. The incident is forgotten – and so, very often, is the heirloom. The wise restorer, having in any case much too much to do, will not even make a start on the job until several phone calls have convinced him of the family's deep attachment to the ruined treasure. If the object is of little but sentimental value, the chances are that it will pass from memory. Every restorer's cellar is full of such waifs. But if he does do the job, gluing will almost always be preceded by degluing.

Apart from poor gluing jobs he may also have to undo repairs half a century old that have broken again or aged badly. One of the operations involved

2
A clean break between two fragments of a Sung vase. They will knit together perfectly.

4
Macrophotograph of an old fracture. The old adhesive makes a fresh gluing impossible.

here will be removing the staples that modern adhesives render superfluous.

First of all, however, he will make a swift analysis of the kind of adhesive used.

A few years back all "amateur" gluing was done with cellulose adhesive, with which it is absolutely impossible to glue pottery correctly. When the piece glued together in this way inevitably turns up at the restorer's, it at least has the merit of being extremely easy to deglue: it only needs to be soaked in acetone (ill. 5). Cellulose adhesive is instantly recognizable by its highly transparent, blistered appearance. The piece is placed in a bowl with some acetone at the bottom and the restorer bathes it thoroughly with the aid of a brush until the fragments come apart of their own accord, without being forced. The softer the ware being treated, the gentler the treatment needs to be. The fragments are left immersed in the acetone for an hour or so (with the bowl covered to stop the acetone evaporating), and the last traces of old adhesive are then removed from the fractured edges with a toothbrush or paintbrush of which the bristles have been cut down to half their length to make them stiffer (ill. 6).

Nowadays excellent epoxy adhesives are available almost everywhere. Marvellously effective when well used, they can be catastrophic in unpractised hands. A poor gluing job done with epoxy resin can be recognized by the fact that it is impossible to undo either with hot water or acetone and by the smooth, yellow appearance of the excess adhesive.

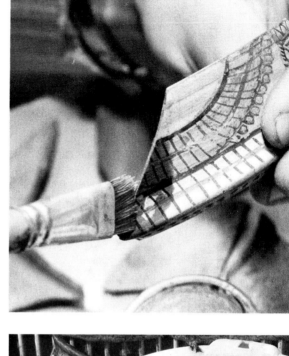

5
A delicate piece of Egyptian pottery being deglued with acetone.

6/7
The remaining traces of cellulose adhesives are removed with brush and acetone.

8
Removing a staple. Notice how the crack has darkened.

The only way of dealing with it is to leave the piece immersed in paint remover; after a few hours – or days, depending on the thickness of the ware – one can hope that the fragments will separate. They are then left to soak in the paint remover for a further period, and the operation is completed by rinsing them well in warm water while brushing them as vigorously as the nature of the ware will allow (i.e. neolithic earthenware very much less vigorously than hard-paste porcelain).

We shall see when we come to the gluing stage that no trace of old adhesive must be allowed to remain. The fractured edges must be examined meticulously and the last specks removed with a graving tool. It is better to have a piece of clay missing from the middle of a fracture than a piece of adhesive that should not be there.

One could mention a number of other adhesives, each one more glutinous and insoluble than the next, but in my experience none of them will stand up long to paint remover.

What appears to be ancient gluing will probably have been done with fish or rabbit-skin glue, both of which dissolve easily in warm water. It may also have been done with shellac, which will dissolve in

9
Chalk deposits being dissolved with hydrochloric acid.

20

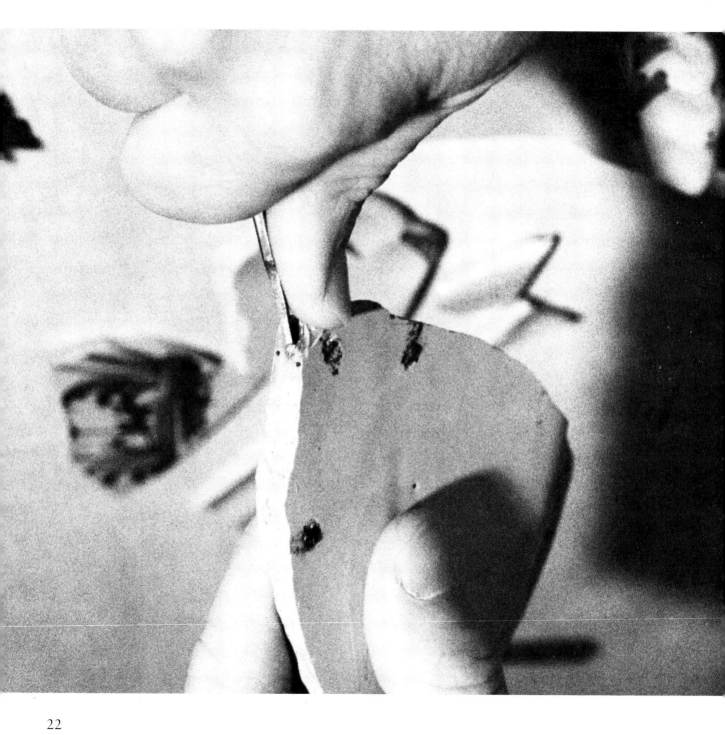

alcohol but softens up enough in hot water to allow the fragments to separate (ill. 7).

While the hot-water method is fine for European porcelain and glazed earthenware, it is out of the question when one is dealing with soft pottery, e.g. archaeological finds, or certain types of ware (Tang, for instance) whose highly devitrified glaze has a tendency to come away from the body. In such cases – common sense will be the judge – only alcohol can be used, and the piece may have to soak for a considerable time.

Once the fragments have separated, the last traces of glue or shellac can be brushed off in alcohol and stubborn bits removed with the graving tool. The darker shade of these ancient types of adhesive stands out clearly against lighter wares.

Nowadays, when your eighteenth-century Sèvres plate is not often used for carving the roast on, most pottery is not repaired with a view to making it proof against washing-up – although of course adhesives have greatly improved and are in particular no longer soluble in water – but for purely decorative purposes. So for both negative and positive reasons restorers have stopped using those hideous staples that once served to make up for the inadequacy of the available adhesives (ill. 8). One very often comes across them on the undecorated backs of pieces of glazed earthenware or porcelain, seldom disfiguring the decoration as in the example illustrated. They can usually be removed quite simply with the aid of a pair of pointed pliers, but

10
Before gluing, the restorer removes a small flake in the body that would have prevented a perfect fit.

extreme care is called for if they offer any resistance. They will of course leave holes lined with rust, which will have to be removed with hydrochloric acid or even scraped off with the graving tool.

Cleaning fractures on archaeological finds

Excavated pottery is soft, porous, and friable – and must be treated accordingly.

Old adhesive can be removed with any of the usual solvents except hot water, but of course greater care is needed than when degluing glazed earthenware and porcelain. Extra special care, for example, is called for when degluing a fragile piece of soft earthenware that has been rapidly and carelessly stuck together at the dig with cellulose adhesive. It will be soaked in acetone and the fragments left to come apart of their own accord; no attempt will be made to pull them apart as the adhesive may prove stronger than the body and bring away a film of earthenware with it. If the solvent reveals that some fragments have been renewed in stucco or plastic, the restorer will be extremely mistrustful as regards using them again. Experience shows that "false teeth" encountered in a poorly glued piece of pottery are dangerous things to use in its restoration, because they will lead to the same errors of gluing. The best thing to do is to put them on one side and only use them, if at all, to put the finishing touches to an otherwise complete job, having no qualms about adjusting them to fit.

A very much trickier problem, however, will be the deposits, particularly chalk deposits, that the fragments may have picked up during their long centuries in the soil (ill. 9).

A good scrub under the tap with a soft brush will get rid of any earth, but chalk deposits will prove much more stubborn. An added complication is that they are not always visible; a very fine deposit may be indistinguishable from the ware and only minute comparison of the fragments by a trained eye and careful study of the grain of the fractured edges will give an accurate idea of its thickness. Sometimes chalk deposits can be scraped off a glaze, but trying to scrape off chalk deposits that sit in the grain of a fracture will only impair the fracture as far as gluing is concerned. Careful use of hydrochloric acid is indicated here, and the restorer will have handy on the bench beside him a large bowl of water containing a few cubic centimetres of alkali as well as a smaller glass container with the acid (the basic vapours will react with the acid vapours to produce impressive white fumes). Acid is applied to the fractured edges with a cotton bud and left until it stops bubbling and the ware has recovered its uniform, pure colour. Usually just wetting a fracture with chalk deposits on it brings out a difference in colour between chalk and ware. The treated fragments are placed in a bowl of weak ammonia water to neutralize the hydrochloric acid.

Poor fractures

Another obstacle to a successful gluing operation, this one irremediable, is when excavated wares have had a rough time underground, as it were, and the fragments have become worn in much the same way as pebbles are worn by the action of the tide. We shall be looking into the problem of wear when we come to deal with gluing and with ways of getting round a poor fracture. All we need say at this stage is that even worn edges need to be scrupulously cleaned.

One last obstacle that sometimes crops up has to do with the texture of the ware itself at the time of breakage. This is flaking. It occurs in certain very soft, thick French faiences, in archaeological finds, and in bevelled fractures in porcelain. Tiny flakes of ware in the middle of the fractured edges come away slightly and prevent the fragments from knitting together correctly (ill. 10). The important thing is to know that this can happen and not to be astonished when two freshly broken fragments show a poor knit. Remedial action is taken at the dress rehearsal stage immediately before gluing; what is needed is a certain flair in identifying the offending spot and a sharply pointed tool with which to remove a little more ware than necessary while taking very great care indeed not to touch the visible edges of the fracture. But this is of course very much a last resort – not that you should think the restorer feels entitled to file down any and every fragment that does not want to fit!

All these things are basically simple and only need to be done carefully, yet experience shows that a piece of broken pottery that has once been badly glued will never make as neat a job as one that comes to the restorer innocent of old adhesive and the efforts of the unversed. The least obstacle will, at the gluing stage, introduce an error that, however tiny at first, will grow and grow as more fragments are glued on until the last fragment is almost bound to project.

Cleaning surfaces

Any good detergent will make a dirty piece of glazed earthenware or porcelain bright and shiny again. Before proceeding to this simple operation, however, the restorer will check whether the piece has been repaired or not. If it is intact, no particular precautions are necessary; if it has been glued and retouched at some time he will do his cleaning with a pad of cotton wool dipped in soapy water, rinsing with another pad dipped in clean water.

Archaeological finds both broken and whole tend for obvious reasons to be positively coated with earth and chalk deposits over the glaze and decoration. The rule here is one that goes for nearly all branches of art restoration: start cleaning with the mildest agent available, use a stronger one if that does not work, use a still stronger one if that does not work, and admit defeat when it looks as if you are beginning to damage the glaze and decoration. So the first stage is gentle brushing with water, which will get rid of the earth and any soluble elements obscuring the decoration. If brushing does not work, it means you are dealing with a chalk deposit. Sometimes the deposit is a thick one and the restorer will try chipping it away; if the glaze is sufficiently smooth and hard and adheres well enough to the ware he can, by attacking the base of the deposit with a sharp tool (a small flat chisel or graver), lift it off without scratching.

Often, however, the deposit is harder than the piece itself and sticks faster to the glaze than the glaze does to the ware, in which case the chipping method might well bring away glaze and decoration as well. The restorer needs a more selective method, one that will attack the deposit while stopping short of

11
A statuette from Myrina with saltpetre damage.

the glaze, and here a small grinding wheel with a flexible drive cable will give good results – provided that the hand of the person using it is as steady as a rock!

A safer but possibly less successful method is to use an ion exchanger of the kind housewives put into the water to soften it for their washing machines. A piece of pottery with a really obstinate chalk deposit can be soaked for a week in distilled water containing ion exchanger without coming to any harm. By then part of the deposit will have disappeared, gentle brushing will remove a good deal more, and the rest will usually be soft enough to be chipped away, as in the first method.

If the deposit still resists, the restorer may rough it down with the carborundum wheel, stopping short of the glaze, and remove the remaining coat by progressive spot applications of pure hydrochloric acid with the aid of a cotton bud, taking care to neutralize the effect of the acid by dipping the object in a bath of slightly alkalized water after cleaning. Great care is needed throughout the operation and the restorer must be in complete control at all times, because of the risk that acid will destroy the calcareous parts of the ware itself. But if the ware has been fired to a sufficient degree of vitrification it will stand up well and the results will be spectacular.

A somewhat similar problem may be encountered in wares with a heavy glaze (Han dynasty wares, for example) that has become partially decomposed through contact with the earth in which they lay buried. Hydrochloric acid in conjunction with a certain amount of gentle scrubbing will reveal how much of the glaze remains unaffected, and what was previously a dull, lustreless piece of pottery will start to gleam with all the inimitable iridescent effects of flakes of devitrified glaze.

Again, though, the greatest care is called for. Every attempt to improve the appearance of a piece can end up by making it look worse. The restorer will always start with a small trial area before tackling the whole: if something goes wrong, the damage can then be covered up. We could formulate another general law of cleaning: set your hopes high, and only come down gradually.

Saltpetre rot

Special treatment is required in the case of certain archaeological finds in which saltpetre has started to form. Such wares will have a strongly saline taste and will exhibit bright white crystals that humidify as soon as there is an increase in relative humidity. Saltpetre rot will eventually destroy the object, if it has not already begun to do so. Different salt concentrations will set up tensions beneath the glaze; this will crack off, and the body will break up into fine flakes until it disintegrates completely. No gluing can be done on a piece of pottery with saltpetre rot.

The treatment required is extremely simple and consists in soaking the piece in distilled water for several days (or weeks, depending on its size), changing the water daily. The saltpetre, dissolving in the water, will be evacuated from the ware by osmosis. The treatment is continued until the water remains soft (this can be checked by applying an electric current to it: a voltmeter will show if the current still passes, i.e. if the water is still saline). After treatment the piece may be extremely friable and require consolidation. Repeated spraying with a tube of cellulose adhesive dissolved in a litre of acetone will do the trick.

II GLUING

A gluing job always starts off well; the trouble comes later – for the uninitiated about half-way through the operation, for the experienced restorer when he gets to the last few fragments. It takes a virtuoso acrobat to glue a broken piece of pottery back together without losing patience and without leaving any unevennesses. The purpose of this chapter is to try to uncover some of the pitfalls encountered and outline a few simple rules that will help make a success of what is after all one of the key operations of restoration.

In view of the care we have taken over removing all foreign bodies from the fracture in order to make the fragments knit together as well as possible (almost as well as if they had never come apart), it will be readily appreciated that the first thing one looks for in a good glue is thinness, i.e. a high adhesion-to-quantity ratio.

But however thin the glue selected, it will still create a certain thickness when applied, and if it is black or red like shellac it will show up as a thin dark line. Consequently restorers have always been on the lookout for colourless, invisible adhesives.

As recently as ten years ago there were not many of them about, and a turn-of-the-century restoration job, even if not disfigured with staples, will always be marred by thick lines of reddish-brown shellac or some other adhesive that has darkened with age. Porcelain restorers were close to despair when they found they could no longer get hold of the swimming-bladders of Danube sturgeon. These used to make an outstanding adhesive – powerful, highly fluid, and completely transparent. The bladders were melted down in water that was kept carefully below boiling-point. The result was then filtered to separate the adhesive from the insoluble animal matter – quite an operation in itself. Finally, since in common with all the animal adhesives used in cabinet-making and book-binding it set not only when dry but also when cold, the fragments to be glued had first to be heated with the blowlamp.

But a fresh product always comes along – proving so much easier to use that one wonders how one ever got anywhere with the old one. And by the time the new panacea has been in use for a couple of months no one can understand how the firm managed to survive for a century without it.

Apart from its exotic origin, Danube sturgeon

swimming-bladder glue, now completely unobtainable, had the additional advantage of being easily soluble in water and hence of qualifying as reversible – an essential requirement as far as museographical restoration is concerned. Today the restorer has to choose between an adhesive that dissolves readily in either water or acetone and a polymerizable adhesive such as one of the epoxy resins or cyanocrylates, which are a great deal stronger but infinitely more difficult to break down and get rid of in the event of the job having to be started all over again. An outstanding restorer of Greek pottery used to go on degluing and regluing until the most difficult job was perfect – and he will have chosen his adhesive accordingly. This is not to disparage polymerizable adhesives, which are capable of rendering great services; they just demand absolute confidence on the part of the restorer in his ability to bring off a perfect piece of gluing.

An important thing is to match the strength of the adhesive employed to that of the material to be glued. It is pointless and dangerous to glue an extremely friable piece of soft-paste pottery with a high-strength adhesive that may come away and bring a layer of ware with it on either side, as has happened in many cases of archaeological finds glued with cellulose adhesive.

A further choice to be made is between a slow-setting and a fast-setting adhesive, depending on whether one wants to glue the whole piece in one go or do it fragment by fragment, letting the adhesive set between each operation.

What is the biggest problem as regards gluing?

Well, to start with, the simplest and most obvious technique is not in fact the right one. Faced with the task of gluing a piece of pottery that has broken into – let us say – thirty pieces, the beginner, regardless of what adhesive he is using, will instinctively glue two fragments together as soon as he finds they fit. He will proceed to reduce the number of fragments and at the same time reconstruct the piece in much the same way as one would put up a wall, allowing the adhesive to set between each series of operations, depending on the stability achieved. The slightest error in gluing two fragments together will be carried over with interest when a third is added. Very soon the fragments will not fit at all, or a crack will refuse to close, and the aspiring restorer will either have to put up with a number of very pronounced unevennesses or begin all over again, which will be extremely difficult in view of the fact that the adhesive has already set.

Correct gluing technique will not eliminate all errors but it will reduce them to the minimum; above all it will cause them to cancel one another out rather than adding up.

The classical technique of gluing pottery is valid for any kind of ware, though certain features will be appropriate to archaeological finds, to glazed earthenware, or to porcelain, and certain more modern techniques such as the systematic use of adhesive tape or the employment of cyanocrylates will simplify matters in particular cases.

12
Modern techniques of gluing glazed earthenware. This piece has been reassembled entirely with the aid of adhesive paper. The actual gluing comes later.

The jig-saw puzzle

The restorer starts by arranging all the fragments on the bench in front of him in such a way as to give himself an overall picture of the way they fit together before he begins gluing them. This may sometimes amount to a veritable jig-saw puzzle (ill. 13), in solving which he will be able to draw on a certain number of aids.

The decoration, if there is one, will be the principle guide to how the fragments fit together, though other important indicators will be the shape of the fragment, the particular segment of sphere or cylinder that it constitutes, variations in the colour of the ware or the glaze, and, in wheel pottery, the lie of the turning marks. For the restorer all this adds up to a fascinating exercise in observation – rendered the more difficult by the fact that classical gluing technique does not allow him to reconstitute the piece fragment by fragment as the latter come to hand, as he could for example with a normal jig-saw puzzle.

The first step, then, is a summary classification of the fragments starting from the centre of the piece to be repaired – the foot of a vase, the middle of a plate or bowl – in order to establish the order in which they are to be glued.

Without letting himself get involved in any extensive gluing at this stage, the restorer may simplify things somewhat by sticking the very tiny fragments to larger ones as he finds where they fit, on the principle that tiny fragments can only introduce tiny errors.

Finding where they fit will of course necessitate a certain number of trial fittings, but since too many of these may impair the quality of the fracture it is advisable to exercise fairly strict restraint in this respect.

Once he has a good idea of where all the fragments belong the restorer can start the reassembly process by trying to reduce the number of elements he has to deal with (ills. 14 and 15). Leaving the very large fragments on one side for the moment, he concentrates on sticking the small and medium-sized ones together in such a way as to end up with about five large composite fragments that knit together well and in which small errors of gluing will still at this stage cancel one another out and disappear. He can then reassemble the piece as a whole in a final gluing operation, making use of various aids such as clamps, rubber bands, and adhesive paper.

Gluing soft earthenware – archaeological finds

We are talking here about primitive pottery that has barely been fired, a priceless piece of Greek pottery, an extremely friable pre-Columbian terracotta – how does one set about gluing something of this kind?

The object is fragile, of documentary value, a museum-piece, and what it needs is a thin, water-soluble, slow-drying adhesive that will above all

13
The jig-saw puzzle.

14/15
The fragments are glued in a particular order. First their number is reduced by gluing the smallest ones to larger ones.

31

not alter the colour of the ware. Formerly restorers used animal glues almost exclusively. The best thing nowadays is a very good polyvinyl acetate or cabinet maker's emulsion adhesive that can be thinned down with water.

This sort of ware is porous, and if a little adhesive with thirty to forty percent water added is applied to a fractured edge the water will be absorbed very quickly, leaving a film of glue of a certain thickness. Moreover the more porous the ware the more quickly this will happen. So the first step is to waterproof the ware.

WATERPROOFING

This is done by brushing all the fragments with a solution of shellac varnish and alcohol.

17
These five fragments should be glued in a single operation.

16
Fragments drying in a sand box.

However, the object of the exercise can be defeated by laying a film on the fractured edge that will then impede precise gluing. The greatest discretion is called for – even at the risk of not obtaining a completely waterproof finish. The criteria are the colour of the ware and whether or not it shines; proper waterproofing will leave the colour unaffected, and shine would indicate the presence of unabsorbed varnish. (There is incidentally an anti-varnishing school that prefers to use a more heavily diluted adhesive on non-waterproofed fractures and act with lightning precision before the water has had time to become absorbed.)

32

18
Missing fragments make a piece difficult to glue together.

A good way of getting round varnishing the fractures is to saturate all the fragments with water before gluing them with polyvinyl acetate. The glue will not be absorbed – but neither will it dry before the whole piece is dry. The piece will have to be reassembled in one go without the advantage of any preliminary gluing, which will call for the use of aids – clamps, string, etc. – to hold the fragments together.

But when all is said and done, varnishing is still the most advisable solution. Once the varnish is dry and the fragments have been arranged in the correct order, gluing can proceed in the ordinary way.

GLUING

The first step is to bring the two fragments together to check the correct position. With a clean fracture this is easy to find, though straight fractures are more difficult to glue in place than curved fractures, which tend to fall into position naturally (ills. 16, 17, 18). Then polyvinyl acetate adhesive thinned down with forty percent water is applied to the fractured edges with a brush that is not likely to shed a hair in the process. The adhesive is not taken quite to the end of the fracture to be glued, the object being to avoid leaving a deposit in the corner that might put the next fragment out of true. And if two fragments form an acute angle the fragment that fills the angle must be found before the first two are glued together; it may be impossible to introduce it afterwards.

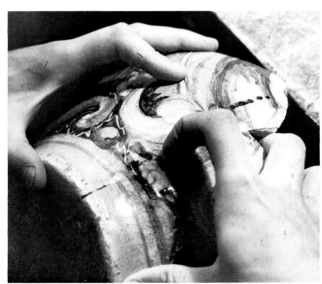

19
It is best to begin with the bottom of the vase.

The adhesive having been applied, the two fragments are held one in each hand and pressed together as hard as possible (within the limits imposed by the strength of the ware concerned). Not to worry about any adhesive that may get squeezed out – that can be wiped off immediately by an assistant standing by with a damp cloth. Or if no assistant is available, the restorer's hands being occupied his tongue will come in very useful both for removing any excess adhesive (polyvinyl acetate is non-toxic) and for detecting any unevenness in the join. A polyvinyl gluing job will hold after a quarter of an hour but will not be really solid until two hours after completion. One can take advantage of this fact by proceeding to further gluing after only a quarter of an hour's drying time; on the other hand any errors that emerge can be corrected by rehumidifying the adhesive before the two hours are up.

20/21
The gluing has been done in a single operation, the restorer has checked that there are no unevennesses, and the vase is now held together with elastic bands while the adhesive sets.

While simplifying the jig-saw puzzle by gluing the tiny pieces to larger ones and the small pieces to other small pieces, the restorer will resist the temptation to go on and complete the job in this way, since if he ended up with two large composite fragments they would almost certainly not fit together. It is better to keep the composite fragments to a reasonable size and then complete the job in a single swift operation once one is down to about five or six of them. A dress rehearsal without adhesive will show which fragments should come when and also indicate the best method of support for when the adhesive is setting – whether rubber bands, spring clips, string, or adhesive tape.

Self-adhesive paper can, as we shall see, be a tremendous help in gluing pottery in that it offers a way of holding the fragments firmly together while the adhesive dries. In the case of archaeological finds, however, it is frequently unusable; either the absence of glaze and the friability of the ware will prevent it from sticking or, if there is a glaze, it will be too weak and there may be a danger of the adhesive tape pulling it away from the body. A glaze should always be tested for strength first. If despite a weak glaze there is no alternative to using adhesive tape, the glaze is best destroyed in advance with the appropriate solvent. Clothes pins, spring clips, screw clamps, and suchlike aids are indispensable for ironing out any obstinate unevennesses. They are placed across the fracture to hold the two fragments in the same plane.

Rubber bands need to be used with care and always in conjunction with the arched effect of a spherical or cylindrical piece. Before the adhesive has set the reassembled object will be armed with judiciously placed rubber bands; the tensile force generated will

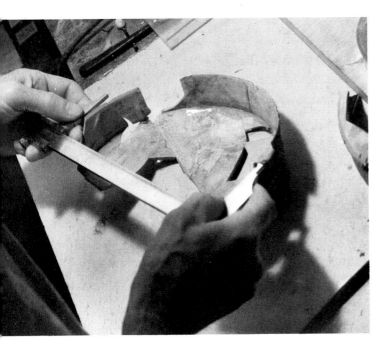

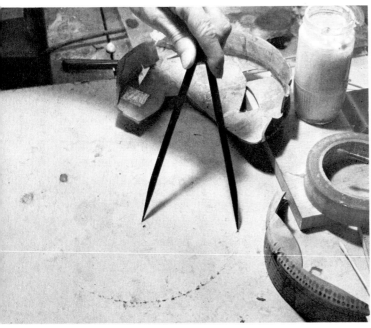

be automatically distributed over the entire surface, resulting in excellent support for the fragments the restorer has urged into place with the strength of his fingers.

String is used only in exceptional cases – for example very large pots that need to be held together very tightly. A loop of string somewhat larger than the pot to be held is twisted with the aid of a stick until it forces the fragments into the correct position. It will have to be an excellent gluing job not to burst apart again when the string is removed. Large pieces of pottery are glued with undiluted adhesive.

Having reduced a mass of splinters to five or six composite fragments, the restorer proceeds to assemble them in a single operation (ills. 20 and 21). This is best done with the aid of an assistant. Applying adhesive quickly (not worrying too much about exactness at this stage) to the fragments forming the base of the centre of the piece, the restorer fits those together first; then, with the assistant holding them in position, he adds the rest of the fragments, working towards the outside and completing the operation by wiping off any excess adhesive and making use of one or more of the methods of fixing just described.

With certain types of cups or relatively flat vessels it is necessary – in spite of what I was saying a moment ago – to reduce the fragments to two. The chances of two large composite fragments fitting together perfectly are virtually nil, but polyvinyl acetate adhesive being slightly elastic, the restorer, taking

22/23
With the aid of a circle drawn to the diameter of the dish, the two fragments can be glued together correctly despite the fact that some material is missing.

advantage of this fact, will be able to force them into the correct position and hold them there with adhesive paper or a clamp.

A Khmer restorer at Angkor in Cambodia, a past master at repairing the large jars dug up by the archaeologists, used to start by gluing the foot of the jar together and winding a piece of string around it; then, as he reassembled the walls of the jar, he would carefully wind the string higher and higher until the completed piece was left to set in a veritable corset consisting of several balls. It was a clever method but at the same time a risky one, because it made it impossible to check the piece for unevennesses.

INCOMPLETE FINDS

Very often excavated pieces are incomplete and the restorer finds himself with only a very small area of contact with which to position a large fragment correctly within the circular plan of the whole. This calls for a certain amount of imagination. The restorer will use flexible rods bent to match the curvature of the piece, and a circle drawn with a pair of compasses on a sheet of cardboard to the diameter of the piece will serve as a further guide (ills. 22 and 23). The fragment will be held in position by means of a plug of some kind (ill. 24).

Even more difficult is positioning a fragment (or group of fragments) that clearly belongs to the piece

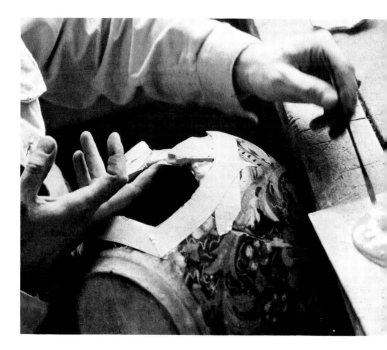

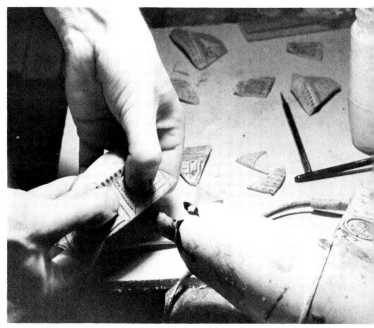

24
Here a piece has virtually nothing round it. It is held in place by means of a polyester plug.

25
A current of warm air makes vinyl adhesive set more quickly. Polyvinyl adhesive can be softened in warm air.

being repaired but offers no point of contact with the other fragments recovered. Curvature and turning marks will help to place it in one dimension, and any decoration the piece may have will be of even greater assistance. Again a certain amount of initiative is required. For example the fragment can be fixed in its presumed position with modelling clay. The restorer fills the entire missing portion from inside with modelling clay (taking care not to get any grease on the outside and on the fractured edges). Being soft but not elastic the modelling clay will hold the fragment in position while the restorer checks with a flexible rod whether it is in the correct plane. He will then fix it there with a rough plaster plug and remove the modelling-clay backing.

If the piece is without decoration the placing of such a fragment is necessarily somewhat arbitrary. In the absence of any precise indication the restorer will put it near one of the edges of the missing portion.

HOT-AIR GLUING

In certain acrobatic gluing jobs on highly friable wares that will take neither rubber bands nor adhesive tape the restorer is sometimes glad if he can virtually weld two fragments by pressing them together with his fingers in a stream of hot air from an electric dryer mounted on his bench or wielded by an assistant (ill. 25). Vinyl adhesive dries in a few minutes.

It is not a good idea to use this method simply to cut down drying time and speed up the reassembly of a piece broken into a large number of fragments, because holding the fragments by hand while the adhesive dries is anything but accurate. But at particularly tricky moments of the operation it will come in useful.

Polyvinyl adhesive, on the other hand, turns soft again in hot air without losing its adhesion – a phenomenon the restorer makes use of to correct any unevennesses that come to light only after the adhesive has set.

GLUING POOR FRACTURES

Sometimes archaeological finds have had such a rough passage that the fractured edges have become worn rather in the manner of pebbles in the sea and no longer knit together properly. It is very difficult to glue such fragments together without leaving any unevennesses.

But while one quite often comes across bad fractures, it is very rare for all the fragments of a piece to be worn in this way. Generally the restorer finds himself with one or two fragments that pose this kind of problem, the balance having cleaner fractures.

Common sense suggests not using worn fragments to start off a gluing job but first gluing other fragments that one is more sure of and adding the worn fragments afterwards. A modelling clay plug will hold them in place while the adhesive sets, and a flexible rod and a good eye will tell whether they are in the correct plane.

Some large earthenware vessels – particularly pre-Columbian wares – are so friable that none of the fractured edges meet completely (ill. 26). For one thing this makes the fragments very difficult to position accurately, and for another normal adhesive has insufficient volume to make up for what is missing. Here the restorer first glues all the fragments about which there is no doubt; then, using a fast-drying polyester tinted to the approximate colour of the ware, he beds the damaged fragments

26
This very friable pre-Columbian terracotta needs a thick adhesive – a polyester.

into place. The polyester sets without any shrinkage and fills the place of the missing material. An equally successful method is to use a mixture of tinted plaster and adhesive; it may be less easy to handle but it matches earthenware more closely. In this case the fractured edges will first be spread with adhesive to make the plaster bond better. The fragments can be held in place by means of a modelling-clay backing inside the piece; the plaster or polyester will then be applied like a fill.

An extreme example of this type of restoration job was a large Greek vase of which none of the fragments was much bigger than a postage stamp and all the fractured edges were completely rounded, so that it was impossible to proceed by positioning each fragment on the basis of the one before. The vase was reassembled as accurately as possible without a drop of adhesive, using only strips of adhesive tape applied to the outside. Well-warmed and softened modelling clay was applied to the inside until the whole vase was completely full. The vase was then placed upside-down on the bench and the adhesive tape carefully removed with alcohol in order not to destroy what was left of the decoration. Then, taking advantage of the fact that modelling clay is soft without being elastic, the restorer minutely adjusted the position of each fragment in turn, which he was able to do because none of them knitted in with its neighbours. Next polyvinyl adhesive was injected into all the cracks, and when it had set all remaining holes were filled with a mixture of tinted whiting and adhesive (see chapter III, FIL-

LING). Finally the vase was turned right side up again and the modelling clay carefully removed with a teaspoon, the last traces being rinsed out with xylene.

EXCESS ADHESIVE

In gluing soft-paste wares and archaeological finds with a light adhesive such as polyvinyl acetate, which in any case will generally be diluted with water, the problem of excess adhesive seldom arises to any extent since this type of adhesive disappears almost completely when dry. If the restorer is lucky enough to enjoy the services of an assistant, he can press the fragments together and have the assistant remove with a small damp sponge any beads of excess glue that are squeezed out of the fracture. But this can always be done after the gluing operation

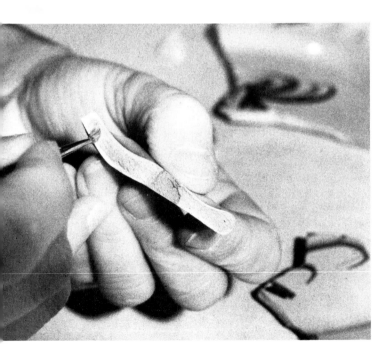

has been completed, provided the reassembled piece is adequately held together with adhesive tape, rubber bands, clamps, and so on.

If there is still excess adhesive in evidence when the piece is dry, it can be softened up with paint remover and peeled away with a sharp tool. Paint remover is only to be used on fairly impermeable glazes, however; on soft, unglazed wares or wares with only a very light glaze it tends to leave indelible traces.

In the case of a worn fracture that needs to be glued with polyester adhesive, a certain amount of polyester will be left bulging above the surface of the piece. It is no good trying to wipe this off because you will only spread it over the surface where it will polymerize for good. Wait until it jells and then, in the brief period when it is still soft enough to cut but already hard enough to hold firm, slice it off with a razor blade. This may not always be possible, however, and the restorer may be faced with the task of removing excess polyester that has already hardened. The method here is to shave it off with a very sharp chisel – bearing in mind, of course, that the reason why polyester was used in the first place was because of the extreme friability of the ware. He will keep the chisel at a low angle to the surface of the piece and take off thin shavings in the direction in which the ware is strongest. He may use a riffler too – taking great care not to touch the surface of the ware.

27
The adhesive is not taken quite to the edge of the fragment.

28/29
The mended plate is held together with adhesive paper and elastic bands until the adhesive sets.

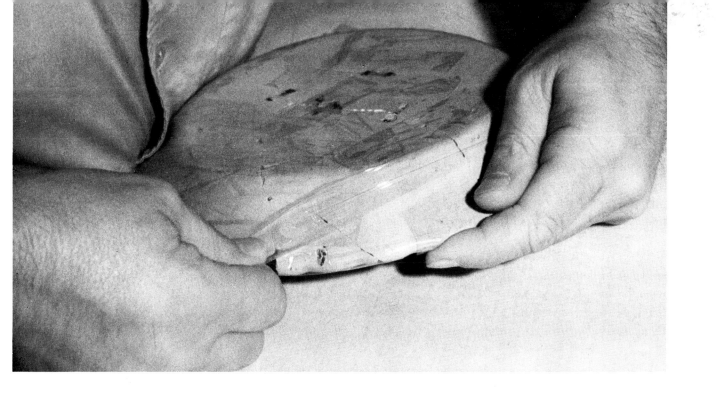

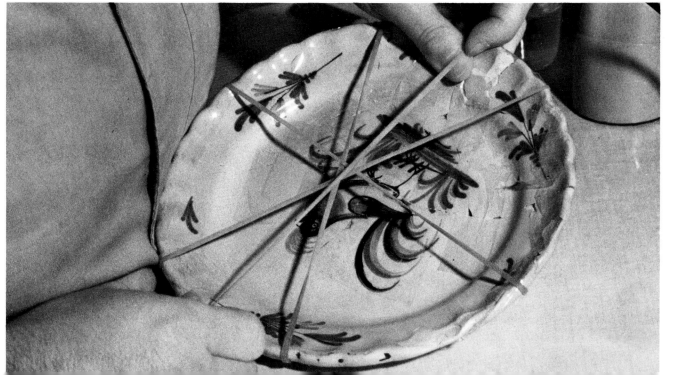

Gluing glazed earthenware

WITH POLYVINYL ADHESIVE

Glazed earthenware glues very well with polyvinyl adhesive; the procedure is the same as for soft-paste wares, permitting extremely delicate work and giving highly satisfactory results. Restorers like the fineness and neatness of polyvinyl adhesive for intricate repairs to small pieces, particularly to certain types of delicate Chinese stoneware.

WITH EPOXY RESINS

In general, however, an epoxy adhesive will be preferred. There are several reasons for this: firstly the hardness of glazed earthenware calls for a rather heavier adhesive than polyvinyl acetate, secondly a piece of glazed earthenware is more likely to be subjected to washing than an archaeological find, and thirdly the usually smooth and shiny glazed surface of this type of ware offers an excellent purchase for adhesive tape, which means that gluing can be done in a single operation with a slow-drying adhesive that allows corrections to be made afterwards.

The fragments are first meticulously cleaned and then dried in a dust-free atmosphere. Meanwhile the restorer will have procured the services of a good assistant, since epoxy resin remains workable for one to two hours, depending on the ambient temperature, and the job needs to be completed

30
Warming the fragment of porcelain will keep the epoxy resin more fluid.

before it starts to set. The assistant's job is to apply the adhesive tape, and he will have a dispenser handy.

The restorer will also have done his jig-saw puzzle very thoroughly and established a fairly precise chronology for the gluing of the fragments, degluing as a result of second thoughts being inevitably prejudicial to the condition of the fractured edges. Selecting two fragments that can be glued together without making it impossible to add a third, the restorer places them together to check whether they knit properly (a small imperfection may be due to flaking, for example, in which case the offending spot will be located and the flake removed with a sharp tool). He goes over the fractured edges once more with a stiff brush to remove any remaining obstacles, then applies epoxy resin with the spatula in a thin line or a series of tiny drops down the middle of one of them, carefully stopping short of the end of the fracture in order to avoid gluing up a corner (ill. 27). He then presses the two fragments together as hard as he can to expel the maximum amount of adhesive and achieve the best possible knit (taking very great care to press in the plane of the two fragments; a skid will have disastrous effects on the fractured edges, and all the tiny fragments will be picked up by the freshly-applied adhesive). If the worst comes to the worst and the fragments do skid apart, however, there is nothing for

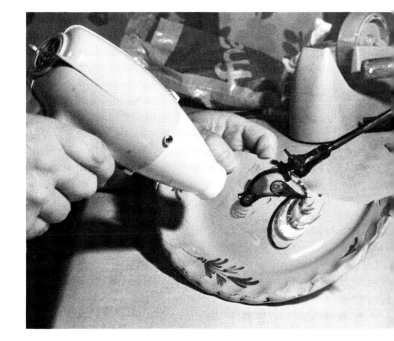

31
A powerful clamp in the right place will eliminate an unevenness.

32
Example of an unevenness.

it but to start again from scratch by cleaning the fractured edges with trichlorethylene.

The fragments are now glued in position and held together by hand. This is where the assistant comes in. Tearing off a strip of adhesive tape, he applies half of it to one of the fragments and goes over it with his fingernail to make it stick to the glaze (ills. 28 and 29). He then pulls on the other end and sticks it to the other fragment. Still holding the fragments in position, the restorer turns them over for a second strip of tape to be applied under the same tension to the back. Long fractures will call for several strips on each side.

Provided you start from the right place – the base if it is a vase or the centre if it is a plate – you can reassemble the entire piece in this way. Any unevennesses left at the end of the process (this applies to any kind of pottery restoration) are best detected by passing a fingernail over the fractures; the fingernail is so sensitive that it will feel the tiniest difference of level. Fingertips are no good here because however clean they are they will have the effect of darkening the cracks. Any unevennesses detected will be eliminated with further applications of adhesive tape or by means of powerful rubber bands or clamps, whereby great care must be taken that eliminating one unevenness does not create another somewhere else. If the shape of the piece allows it may be virtually corseted with rubber bands.

Any adhesive squeezed out of the cracks between the strips of tape can be removed at this stage with trichlorethylene.

The piece is then left to set in a warm, dry, dust-free atmosphere. After twenty-four hours the strips of adhesive tape are removed and any excess adhesive left beneath them dissolved with paint remover (which must be thoroughly rinsed off afterwards). A very high degree of cleanliness is needed when gluing with epoxy resin. The workshop must be dust-free, the bench perfectly clean, and the restorer's hands thoroughly washed. Epoxy adhesive remains tacky for almost twenty hours at normal temperatures, and there is a danger of the cracks collecting dirt.

Distortion

A big hindrance in gluing glazed earthenware (and even more in gluing porcelain) is the distortion that sometimes occurs after breakage.

Take the example of a flat plate that has broken in two more or less along its diameter (ills. 31 and 32). Breaking releases the tension set up in the piece as the clay dried or as it was fired or cooled down. As a result the two fragments no longer match exactly; one of them has twisted slightly, so that although the fracture is otherwise perfect the fragments only knit together perfectly at one end, the other being out of true. Levelling them up will only put the first end out of true. This generally occurs in pieces broken into a small number of fragments; with a large number such distortions are more likely to cancel one another out.

Distortion is sometimes extremely difficult to correct. It is a question of recreating the original internal tension – which epoxy resin will then maintain

33
Gluing with cyanocrylates. The vase is assembled with the aid of adhesive paper.

provided it has some support while setting. The restorer above all needs to be familiar with the phenomenon; he will then be able to make the best use of the means at his disposal (clips, small hand vices, adhesive tape, rubber bands, etc.).

A fast-setting thixotropic polyester has been used successfully to help eliminate distortion between two fragments of a large plate (monumental masons' suppliers now stock polyesters that polymerize completely in two to three minutes). The method of procedure is as follows:

The restorer spreads adhesive along the fractured edges and brings the two fragments together, pressing one end of the fracture into position without worrying about the other end being out of true. The glued end is reinforced with adhesive tape on front and back. Then two sizeable lumps of polyester are laid across the fracture between the strips of tape; they perform the same function as the tape but to very much greater effect. Once the polyester has hardened the other end of the fracture can be forced into the correct plane and held there with a small hand vice or two more lumps of polyester. If the deformation reappears in the middle of the fracture it can be corrected by the same means. When the adhesive is thoroughly dry the polyester can be removed with a hot soldering iron.

34
This is a two-person job: one holds the fragments tightly together and the other applies the adhesive paper.

35
The vase is entirely reconstituted before a drop of adhesive is applied.

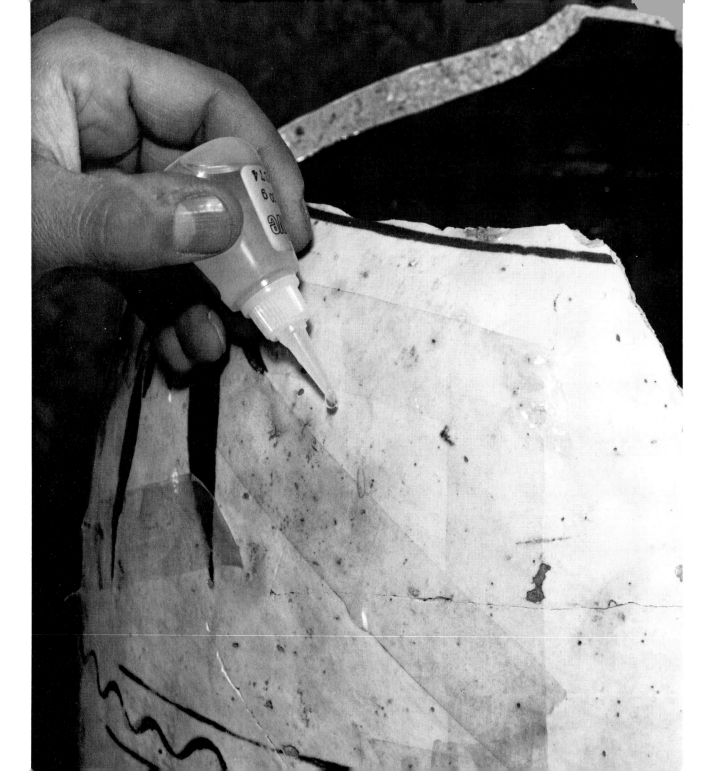

Cyanocrylate adhesives

I have already pointed out how the thickness of the film of adhesive constitutes a serious obstacle to perfect gluing. Restorers have always dreamed of being able to reassemble a vase without getting their fingers sticky or soiling the fractured edges – and then introduce the adhesive afterwards.

With the advent on the market of cyanocrylates this dream is well on the way to fulfilment. The technique of gluing glazed earthenware in particular is undergoing a revolution. It should, however, be pointed out that the properties of this extraordinary family of adhesives are not necessarily all positive.

For one thing the restorer needs to be absolutely clear in his mind as to what he wants to achieve in any particular case, because cyanocrylate adhesive is incompatible with the slightest improvisation. It is a good idea to make a study of its capricious behaviour on such simple gluing jobs as teacup handles, noting in particular that it may set in five minutes or in a quarter of a second, depending on the way in which it is used, the porosity of the ware concerned, and the humidity of the atmosphere (water being the catalyst that makes it polymerize).

Another thing to remember is that a poor cyanocrylate gluing job is virtually impossible to deglue; it may come apart in boiling water but the traces of adhesive will be extremely difficult to remove. The inexperienced restorer, seduced by the perfection of his first cyanocrylate join, may be emboldened to continue reassembling a piece on the wall-building principle, in which case his doom will be sealed;

about the tenth or eleventh fragment will refuse to fit snugly, and he will find himself cursing this merciless deceiver.

The following technique should – theoretically – rule out any possibility of error:

Leaving the adhesive on one side for the moment, the restorer will quietly reassemble the whole piece, however many fragments it is in, with the sole aid of adhesive tape dispensed by an assistant, as when gluing with epoxy resin. He can have second thoughts, he can go back and do a bit again, his time is his own to complete the puzzle in peace. If he is restoring a vase, for example, he can start from the bottom upwards and from the neck downwards until he has two composite sections that may knit together well or may not: it does not matter, because the adhesive tape will have enough give to allow the necessary adjustments at the join and on the rest of the piece, and a strip can always be removed or retightened here and there. The vase can then be held together tightly with rubber bands to close up all the fractures.

The restorer now proceeds to sound the vase all over with his knuckle; if a place sounds hollow it means that a fracture has play and the adhesive tape needs tightening.

This is where the cyanocrylate adhesive comes in. The assistant applies it to all the cracks not covered with adhesive tape while the restorer improves the function of the latter by squeezing hard in the appropriate direction, having made a final check for unevennesses with his fingernail. When adhesive has been applied to all the cracks the vase will be glued – and glued well. The rubber bands and adhesive tape are then removed and glue applied to the portions of the cracks previously covered.

36
Adhesive is applied to the cracks.

The restorer will first try to chip off the excess adhesive with a flat graver, but if this method looks like taking off the glaze too he will use paint remover, which will soften the adhesive without impairing the bond.

If the piece has broken in such a way that numbers of tiny fragments are associated with larger ones, these can be preglued with a drop of adhesive to simplify reassembly.

It goes without saying that cyanocrylates are taboo as far as gluing soft-paste wares such as archaeological finds is concerned. For one thing they are far too powerful and for another they would discolour the ware by rehydrating it. They should be used strictly as described above.

Gluing porcelain

This same method was employed for a while for gluing non-porous hard-paste wares such as porcelain — until some of the pieces glued in this way unexpectedly came apart again. What had happened was that in many cases, particularly if the fractures were clean and the piece skilfully reassembled, the adhesive had failed to penetrate right through the crack.

So epoxy resin is indicated here as it is with glazed earthenware — but with even greater stress on the importance of cleanliness during the operation, porcelain being of course semi-transparent.

If, however, a dress rehearsal on a small number of fragments shows conclusively that the job is going to be very easy, cyanocrylate adhesive may be used in the normal way, i.e. a few drops are placed on the fractured edges (but not spread) and the fragments are brought together with a steady hand. But the hand has to be rock-steady — and one of the things the restorer has to know is his own limitations.

Cracked and distorted pieces

One frequently comes across a piece of pottery — it may be soft-paste or hard-paste ware — in which an incipient crack, by partially releasing the internal tension, has given rise to an unevenness. Very often the only thing to do is to complete the fracture in order to able to glue it up again.

On archaeological finds with this type of damage, however, the crack can sometimes be reduced by pressing the edges together tightly with the fingers. If it can be held in this position by means of rubber bands, clamps, or loops of string, the restorer can try releasing it again, forcing polyvinyl acetate adhesive (diluted with water in proportion to the size of the piece) into the fracture under some kind of pressure, and then clamping it up again until the adhesive has set.

Cyanocrylate adhesives, because they set so fast and because they are so fluid as to penetrate the tightest crack, are marvellously suitable for this type of repair (though for porous soft-paste wares and in particular for archaeological finds they are not recommended as they may stain). The restorer presses the edges of the crack together while an assistant applies a cyanocrylate adhesive all along its length; the crack must then be held closed until the adhesive has set. Or if the crack is an easy one to close the adhesive can be applied to the exposed parts of the fracture before this is done. The setting time of cyanocrylate adhesives varying very greatly according to the dampness of the ware and the humidity of the atmosphere, the restorer has to learn by experience to guess how long it will be in each particular case – whether, for example, it will be longer than his fingers can maintain pressure on the fracture. There is a solidifying agent (though it is not readily obtainable) that can be poured onto the freshly-applied adhesive and will make it set immediately. Using this the restorer can even glue a crack in stages, fixing it point by point with successive applications of adhesive and solidifying agent. Nevertheless there are cases where its use is not recommended; it may get underneath certain types of very porous earthenware glaze and become visible, or it may have side-effects on the glazes used in any subsequent retouching. Another way of cutting down the setting time is to use water as a catalyst, e.g. by very slightly dampening the ware before closing the crack.

Unfortunately, however, in spite of these advances a distorted crack is sometimes very tricky to repair. Dirt, earth, and chalk deposits on archaeological finds and flaking on other types of ware may all get in the way of a satisfactory job.

Before going as far as to extend the crack into an actual break the restorer, having detected the presence of such an obstacle, will attempt to remove it by any means that is not likely to create fresh obstacles. This generally involves the use of water or some other liquid under pressure: it can either be blown through the crack or the vessel can be filled with it in the hope that in flowing out through the crack it will take the foreign body with it. The best thing is one of those little water-compressor appliances that are sold for cleaning the teeth and gums.

Only when all such efforts have failed is there a case for provoking a complete fracture – after which the fractured edges can of course be cleaned in the normal way. Chalk deposits, for example, that may have formed in the crack over several centuries can hardly be removed by any other method. But that does not stop it being the last resort.

One might sum up this survey of modern gluing techniques by listing four final ingredients of success in what is a vitally important part of the restoration process: enormous composure, a precise idea – in advance – of what each stage of the operation will involve, ruling out any necessity for improvisation, a determination not to accept the slightest imperfection, no matter how tiny, and a wise choice of technique, leaving room for second thoughts.

The restorer who scrupulously observes all these points will have no need to fall back on the two crimes that so tragically often deface restored pottery: when degluing old repair jobs one all too frequently comes across one or two pieces – the last to have been glued – that one's predecessor literally filed down to make them fit into a hole too small for them, or else one finds that he took up the same tool to eliminate a stubborn unevenness, destroying both glaze and decoration over an area of several square centimetres. Modern techniques combined with a severely disciplined approach will remove the necessity for such drastic expedients.

III FILLING

Occasionally – if for example the piece to be repaired has absolutely clean fractures, or if the repair is for museographical purposes and as such calls for restraint – the restorer may content himself with a perfect gluing job, leaving no trace of adhesive visible, nor any chips missing, and not worrying about the inevitable hair lines.

More often, though, he has to go on to perform the tedious and difficult operation of filling. This indispensable preliminary to retouching involves replacing with plaster or some other material the chips of clay, earthenware, or porcelain that disappeared in the dustpan or were simply too small to be reused. Or it may be more extensive, involving the replacement of a whole fragment several centimetres square, or renewing the missing neck of a vase, or – and here the restorer needs to be an archaeologist as well – reconstituting an entire vessel on the basis of a few excavated fragments. If retouching is going to consist in imitating the original glaze of the piece, filling will consist in producing an imitation of the body supporting that glaze, in other words an imitation of the actual fired clay; the restorer will be concerned to match the hardness or softness of the latter, its degree of opacity or transparency, its colour, and its texture, since all of these things will affect any subsequent retouching.

If his aim is a restoration detectable only by ultraviolet or X-ray photography, his filling work will have to be perfect – as absolutely smooth as the surface of the surrounding ware and absolutely flush with it. Above all he will need to take enormous pains over his rubbing-down technique; rubbing-down calls for limitless patience and must be done extremely slowly in order to avoid scratching the original glaze at the edges of the filling.

Filling small holes

SOFT EARTHENWARE – ARCHAEOLOGICAL FINDS
For purely archaeological and museographical purposes, certain types of everyday utensil, seen rather as material for study than as vehicles of aesthetic emotion, will require no more than gluing, provided they are complete; the restorer will make

no attempt to disguise the fractures, which on this type of piece are generally worn or otherwise damaged. But on a splendid painted bowl from Greece or a piece of zoomorphic ware from Peru with its rich, vibrant finish a network of fractures – sometimes quite dense – may spoil the harmony of form and decoration. Such a piece needs retouching, which means it must first be filled. And since soft earthenware is usually coloured, the restorer will prepare a fairly soft, coloured fill.

Whiting is placed in a jar together with the necessary pigments (see chapter IV RETOUCHING): red ochre, yellow ochre, umber, a dash of cobalt blue (only these four colours are used). The jar is then closed and shaken like a cocktail shaker, this being the best method of achieving a homogeneous mixture. Adjusting the quantities of pigment and whiting to produce the shade required, the restorer will then check this by mixing up a small quantity of the powder with a weak solution of polyvinyl adhesive and water, drying it with hot air, and comparing it with the body to be matched. It should come as close as possible to the colour of the heart of the earthenware, erring if at all on the light rather than the dark side.

The powder is carefully and thoroughly worked into a paste with the help of a spatula and a glass palette and the addition of water with a small amount of polyvinyl adhesive dissolved in it. It is difficult to give the exact proportions: too much adhesive will result in too hard a filling, tricky to rub down without damaging the surrounding glaze; too little adhesive will make the fill too soft and liable to rub down to below the surface of the piece. On the other hand the proportions of water and adhesive will vary according to the hardness of the

ware being matched; a piece of glazed earthenware will call for a harder fill than a neolithic terracotta, and porcelain an even harder one than that.

A useful trick dates from when restorers employed warm glue as a binding agent. They used to knead the fill by hand, make a sausage of it, hold one end about forty centimetres above the palette, and let it draw itself out. If during the first part of the operation it stuck to the hands there was too much glue in it; if the sausage broke before reaching the palette there was too little. Much used by wood gilders, for example, in preparing their special type of ground, the technique is equally suitable for fill made with a simpler binding agent such as polyvinyl adhesive. The fill is applied with the spatula and forced into all the cracks and tiny holes without the restorer worrying at this stage about perfectly reconstituting the surface of the ware (rubbing-down will do that). It is important always to put on a little too much in order not to have to add more after rubbing-down. Even so, it is a good idea to be prepared for the worst and to keep any leftover fill wrapped in a damp cloth in an airtight container until the job is dry and rubbing-down satisfactorily completed. But while making sure he applies a little too much fill, the restorer will also take care not to cover too much of the surrounding glaze. Rubbing-down

37
The fill is being levelled off with a razor blade and will be rubbed smooth with glasspaper.

38
Filling small gaps in a Greek vase. The fill has been tinted to the exact shade of the ware.

always involves a certain amount of risk to neighbouring areas and one wants to reduce it to the minimum.

The purpose of rubbing-down is to remove the excess fill and so make the filling match the surface of the original ware. It is not difficult to imagine the problems involved in bringing hardened fill down to the level of the very fragile glaze usually encountered on archaeological finds without inflicting any damage on the latter. The job needs to be done slowly and with the right abrasive.

A simple precaution – and one that, needless to say, is all too rarely taken – is to protect the surrounding areas with adhesive tape before one starts filling (provided, of course, that the glaze is solid enough to take adhesive tape and the tape will stick). The excess fill can then be removed very rapidly with a fairly coarse sandpaper (180–200) and there will be no risk of scratching the glaze. When he gets down to the tape the restorer removes it and finishes the job off with a very fine sandpaper.

The sandpaper should be rolled into a small cylinder or folded into a wad and it should be applied only to the filling itself. Right at the end, however, when it is impossible not to touch the edges of the filled area, the restorer will brush them as lightly as he can in the direction of the turning marks. Apart from this there are no secrets – except perhaps that one should reckon to take as much skin off one's fingers as one takes off excess fill.

Taking the example of a Greek black-figure vase, if the restorer has paid particular attention to matching his fill for colour he may be able to confine any retouching to the black figures and leave his fillings in the red portions as they are. He will have deliberately made them a shade lighter than they should be, knowing that a light, clear shellac varnish applied for lustre will darken them by just the right amount. The earthenware may of course not be quite uniform in colour all over the piece, in which case several different shades of fill will be required (see chapter IV RETOUCHING).

Some restorers of black-figure or red-figure vases have gone as far as to treat the black parts with black fill and the red parts with earthenware-coloured fill, doing no retouching but simply rubbing down and applying virgin wax to give a gentle gloss. The black fill needing to be mixed with plumbago to give the requisite metallic finish, it has to be bound with rubber varnish rather than with polyvinyl adhesive, which only binds with whiting. One never gets an invisible restoration job by this method, but it is clean and neat and for restoring classical pottery it constitutes the ideal technique. Unfortunately it can only be used when the black figures are sufficiently opaque not to let the body show through. On many Greek wares, particularly red-figure wares, the black parts are slightly transparent and sometimes have a greenish tinge. Here the fill must match the earthenware and the filled area be suitably retouched (see chapter IV RETOUCHING).

Filling opaque and glazed wares – glazed earthenware and stoneware

The usual method of filling glazed earthenware and stoneware is exactly the same as that used for soft earthenware except that, to match the lighter shade and harder quality of the former, a little less pigment is added to the whiting and a little more adhesive to the water. Rubbing down is less tricky with a tougher glaze, and a coat of clear shellac varnish will complete the operation by waterproofing and hardening the rubbed-down fill.

Here some restorers favour rubbing-down with water (impossible on soft earthenware) on the grounds that it takes less time and they never scratch the glaze. Once the fill is dry they start working on it with the type of abrasive paper that can be used wet, whereby the excess material is more dissolved than rubbed away (ills. 39 and 40). Stopping when he gets near the level of the glaze, the restorer allows the fill to dry again. The rest he rubs down dry, working very gently, and he then varnishes the filled areas to harden them and make them waterproof. This done, he can wash the piece down with water, for it will be completely white by now from the dissolved fill. Wet abrasion is so easy and goes so fast that if one is not careful one soon gets down below the level of the surrounding glaze, creating a hollow that then has to be filled. This can be done by applying a very thin solution of the fill with a brush and rubbing down dry afterwards.

FILLING WITH FAST-SETTING EPOXY RESIN

Nowadays, if a job does not involve too much filling the restorer can use a fast-setting epoxy resin. It will be harder and take longer to rub down than a whiting fill, but it will provide a better-matching ground for retouching, being extremely homogenous, highly adhesive, and both flexible and hard at the same time (ill. 42). It is above all used for repairing cracked edges, where a whiting fill is very delicate as well as being difficult to shape. To save time, part of the excess fill can be removed with the aid of a small grinding-wheel on a flexible drive cable.

FILLING WITH POLYESTER

Other modern techniques can be adapted successfully to suit specific cases. Certain large stoneware vases of the Sung dynasty, for example, have a milky glaze that is fairly thick, irregular, and very slightly translucent (ill. 43). Since the traditional type of filling with whiting would necessitate retouching a much larger area than that filled, restorers prefer to try and match the glaze in a single operation by using coloured thixotropic polyester. This is a high-quality clear polyester of the type sold for setting insects thixotroped with a small quantity of silica and coloured by means of a suitable white colouring agent (sold with it) and a few powder pigments. Care must be taken when mixing it with its catalysts not to use too much cobalt octoate, which would affect the colour.

Once it has set the excess material is removed with a grinding-wheel – also very effective for imitating the irregularities of the original glaze. Retouching will be confined to some slight transparent correction of the filled area and the addition of a few spots.

FILLING TO MATCH THE GLAZE COLOUR

One particular case needed to be filled not to the colour of the body but to the colour of the glaze. It was a large midnight-blue Nevers vase decorated in white and it had broken into more than a hundred fragments. Once glued together, it had in several places, particularly around the point of impact, so dense a network of chips and little holes that filling to the colour of the body and retouching by overpainting in blue would have involved covering up a large area of the glaze completely and redoing all the decoration – of course losing the verve and freshness of the original in the process. As one of a

39
Filling gaps in an Italian vase. The whiting is forced into the cracks.

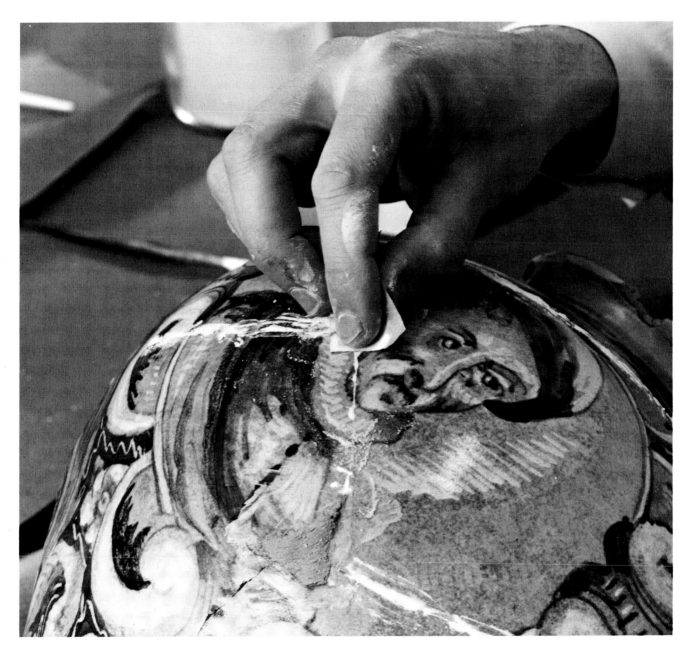

40
Rubbing-down must be done very carefully to avoid scratching the glaze.

pair the vase played an important decorative role in the museum where it was exhibited, so it was decided to compromise by using a blue fill (with rubber varnish as binding agent) that, once rubbed down and varnished, matched the colour of the rest of the glaze. The white decoration was completed on the filled areas. This is a technique that can only be used on wares with highly opaque glazes – and provided one is not after complete invisibility.

RECESSED FILLINGS

Certain glazes on turn-of-the-century wares or Japanese tea-ceremony wares are so thick as to cover the body with a layer up to several millimetres in depth. Here the restorer will recess his fillings by the thickness of the glaze, leaving himself room to reconstitute the latter in some kind of plastic without having to overlap the still-intact glaze, which would make it opaque. In a very small chip it may be only glaze that is missing, in which case the restorer will not fill with tinted whiting but will in effect retouch with a translucent plastic matching the glaze for colour (see chapter IV RETOUCH-ING).

FILLING PORCELAIN

Porcelain is a hard, impermeable, translucent type of ware. From the hard-fired stonewares of the Sung

41
The slightly lighter fill is already very close in colour to the rest of the piece. It will be a simple job to match it up.

42
Some of the larger chips in the edge of this plate are being filled with quick-drying epoxy resin.

60

dynasty it progressed in refinement almost to the translucency of opaline – at which point it is virtually non-repairable.

It is always relatively easy to camouflage a repair to an opaque material. Rather more of a problem with translucent materials – white marble, alabaster, porcelain – it becomes totally impossible in the case of transparent materials such as glass and crystal.

In porcelain, the normal type of filling using whiting or fast-setting epoxy resin will create opaque areas. Even if subsequent retouching achieves a subtle transition between opacity and translucency, such repairs will always show up against the light. Restorers have consequently been tempted to replace missing matter in porcelain with some material that can be applied in the liquid or semi-liquid state and left to harden and that will then have the same translucency as the surrounding ware. One can get pretty close to the look of porcelain with a high-quality polyester judiciously tinted with white. For small fillings, however, the result obtained with this technique is not worth the effort; porcelain and polyester having different indices of refraction, the joins will inevitably be visible and one will end up retouching the entire area anyway – in which case one might as well have used whiting in the first place.

On the other hand this method can be extremely useful when the restorer would rather not retouch. Camouflaging a repair to a piece of fine white porcelain involves retouching very much more than just the filled area, and there may not be enough material missing to justify going to such trouble. Small chips out of the edge of a plate, for example, will be filled with polyester, carefully rubbed down, and then rotten-stoned to give them the gloss of porcelain without using varnish. No further attempt at disguisement is made, and the result is a discreet and elegant piece of restoration.

But where this type of filling becomes really interesting is of course when it comes to renewing whole fragments or missing elements in porcelain ware.

43
The highly specific glaze of this Sung vase has been partially imitated in the polyester fill.

Renewing missing fragments

SOFT EARTHENWARE — ARCHAEOLOGICAL FINDS

Very often with this type of ware the restorer is called upon to renew entire fragments that have become lost or were never dug up in the first place (ill. 44). This may involve anything from filling gaps of one to two square centimetres to, at the other extreme, reconstituting whole vessels on the basis of no more than a few authentic fragments, as was done at Iraklion.

The first operation – this applies to all types of ceramic ware – is to make a mould or support of some kind that will mask the hole to be filled and provide a backing for the fill (stucco, in the case of soft earthenware).

If the hole is not too large the restorer makes a simple support of adhesive paper inside or underneath the piece being repaired, depending what it is. In doing so he takes care that his improvised shuttering does not project inside the hole: it is better to have to remove excess fill than add more. If the hole is larger, modelling clay is used for the shuttering. This is applied carefully to the inside of an intact portion of the vessel in successive layers about a centimetre thick until a rigid block is obtained; the block is then swivelled round to mask the missing portion.

If there is more material missing than is left intact the restorer can proceed in several stages, moving the modelling-clay support on after each lot of poured fill has set.

The support is always applied to the least interesting side of the piece – the inside of a crater or vase, the back of a plate, and so on. Tremendous precision could be obtained, on condition that the shape of the piece was absolutely mechanical and perfectly circular, with more sophisticated shuttering materials than modelling clay. In fact, though, only a fairly rough form of shuttering is needed, hand, eye, and callipers collaborating to perfect the repair afterwards by removing excess or applying additional fill.

If the hole to be filled is in a narrow-necked vase – so narrow that the restorer cannot get his hand through to shutter it from inside with modelling clay or adhesive paper; using fairly stiff plaster, he will try to renew the missing fragment without benefit of shuttering. A less acrobatic and more elegant solution, however, is to provide some kind of temporary shuttering. The vase can be stuffed with tissue paper, for example, which can be removed with forceps afterwards. Or another good trick is to inflate a balloon inside the vessel, deflating it again once the fill has set.

If the piece is completely sealed – a Chinese pillow, for example – or almost completely, like one of those little Corinthian vases with the very narrow neck, the restorer may pack it with very fine sand, leaving a hole in his renewed fragment large enough for the sand to run out of but small enough to be plugged easily afterwards.

If the piece is perfectly cylindrical or conical the shuttering can be made very simply with a sheet of cardboard covered all over with adhesive tape, the back of which will not stick to the fill, whether plaster or polyester.

One will occasionally, like the excellent restorers of

44
This excavated vase has been only partially reconstituted, since the restorer could not legitimately invent the rest of the shape.

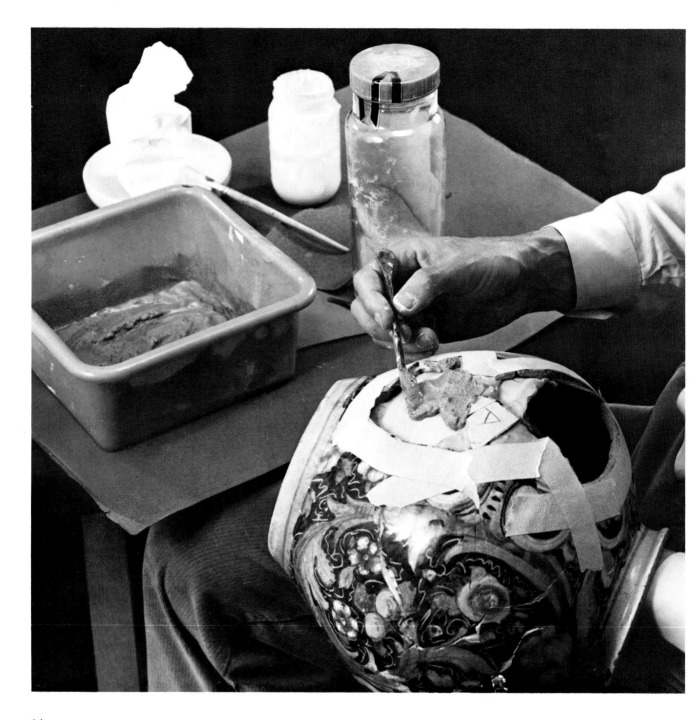

so much Cretan ware, be called upon to reconstitute seventy-five percent of a piece of pottery. This is of course very much more difficult, the few surviving fragments giving no immediate idea of what the piece looked like intact. Here the restorer must combine the skills of archaeologist and geometrician to work out the shape of the original vessel on the basis of the curvature of the few fragments that are left.

Not knowing how the Cretan restorers went about it, one would suggest carving a block of expanded polystyrene to the assumed shape of the inside of the vase; the fragments are then glued together, if they go together, or glued in the appropriate places in relation to one another on the block. The rest is filled in with stucco and patiently rubbed down, and when the vase has been satisfactorily reconstituted the polystyrene core is dissolved out with paint remover.

It goes without saying that none of these shuttering techniques represents the last word on the subject; there is plenty of room for imagination, and the individual restorer will undoubtedly have his contribution to make towards further progress in this field.

Here too I would stress the wisdom of protecting the area around the missing portion before applying any kind of shuttering. There is always a great deal of excess fill to be filed, sliced, or rubbed away afterwards, and any carelessness at the rubbing-down stage will be even more disastrous for the surrounding glaze and decoration than in the case of small fillings. The best thing is to stick adhesive paper or elastoplast all round the edges and use a razor blade to cut out the exact shape of the hole to be filled. The restorer thus provides himself with a perfectly prepared field of operations as well as a valuable alarm signal when, in rubbing-down, he begins to reach the protective surround. On the other hand he need be less anxious about overlapping the edges slightly when applying the fill.

Missing portions in excavated soft earthenware are filled with fine plaster tinted with powdered pigments and worked into a paste with the addition of water and some polyvinyl adhesive. The tinting is done in the manner described for whiting as used for small fillings, the dry ingredients being shaken together in a sealed jar and small quantities mixed up for colour tests (the addition of adhesive may have a slightly darkening effect).

Once he has got the colour about right the restorer prepares his stucco fill by sprinkling the tinted plaster into the polyvinyl acetate-and-water solution. If he has a number of fragments to renew (he might, for example, be dealing with all the pottery found during a dig) he will be wise to mix up a stock of plaster to the same shade and prepare a large quantity of adhesive solution in order to keep his fill constant as regards quality and colour. The amount of adhesive used here is relatively small; two or three centimetres of adhesive in the bottom of a litre of water will be enough to give a solid but still workable stucco.

The batch can be made up in a rubber or flexible nylon bowl. Plaster is sprinkled in until it begins to break the surface of the water; the stucco is then gently worked smooth with a palette knife or broad

45
Filling a large gap in an Italian vase with plaster. Notice the white modelling-clay backing inside the hole.

wooden spatula (mixing too violently will kill the plaster). Before making his filling the restorer coats the fractured edges around the area to be filled with a little undiluted adhesive. When the stucco has thickened sufficiently to be applied without running (a question of catching it at just the right moment), the restorer spreads it in the hole, taking care not to form any air bubbles.

Still keeping an eye on the setting process, and before removing the modelling-clay shuttering, he will remove as much as he can of the excess fill, carving the filled portion to the correct profile, before the stucco hardens completely. This can be done throughout the setting process with a variety of sharp tools – scrapers, gouges, chisels, gravers, etc. Once the stucco is dry, rubbing-down is completed with rasp and sandpaper. One thing that may happen during the operation is that the stucco fragment, shrinking slightly as it sets, may come unstuck (an edge repair on the neck of a vase almost certainly will). This does not matter in the least. The restorer simply reglues it and, when the adhesive has completely set, continues rubbing-down.

Plaster will never give as smooth and perfect a surface as whiting. This will hardly matter in the case of a piece of neolithic ware, but if one is restoring a particularly fine Greek vase a better finish may be desirable. This can be achieved as follows: once the plaster is thoroughly dry and its rubbing-down completed, it is given a thin coat of clear shellac varnish to waterproof it; then a little of the whiting fill that the restorer has been keeping in a damp cloth since filling the smaller holes is applied to the surface of the renewed portion with spatula and brush, allowed to dry, rubbed down, and varnished in its turn.

RENEWING FRAGMENTS ON GLAZED EARTHENWARE

Excellent restorations of glazed earthenware have been and are still carried out in stucco, which was long the panacea of restorers. The procedure is the same as with soft earthenware, except that here the stucco is often left white; it is also mixed up with a little more adhesive to make it harder and, as such, a better match for glazed earthenware.

Nowadays, missing fragments of glazed earthenware are generally renewed with some kind of plastic that will have a similar ring and will give a solid, perfect repair. Before embarking on the renewal of a large fragment with polyester or epoxy resin, however, it is as well to remember that these materials become extremely hard and that the job of bringing a rough plastic filling up to the flawless polish of a piece of faience may be a long and laborious one, involving considerable risk to the surrounding glaze.

White-tinted polyester is excellent, indeed virtually indispensable for repairing the edge of a plate or the neck of a vase (ills. 47–51), plaster not being strong enough for fragments that are only supported on one side. Polyester will make a very good match with the original material, whether earthenware or stoneware, and it will be easier to give it either a flawless finish or the uneven, pitted surface characteristic of certain glazes. This will in turn make retouching very much simpler.

But for filling a really big hole in, for example, an Italian majolica vase, one will quite rightly hesitate

46
The liberally-applied plaster is smoothed off while setting.

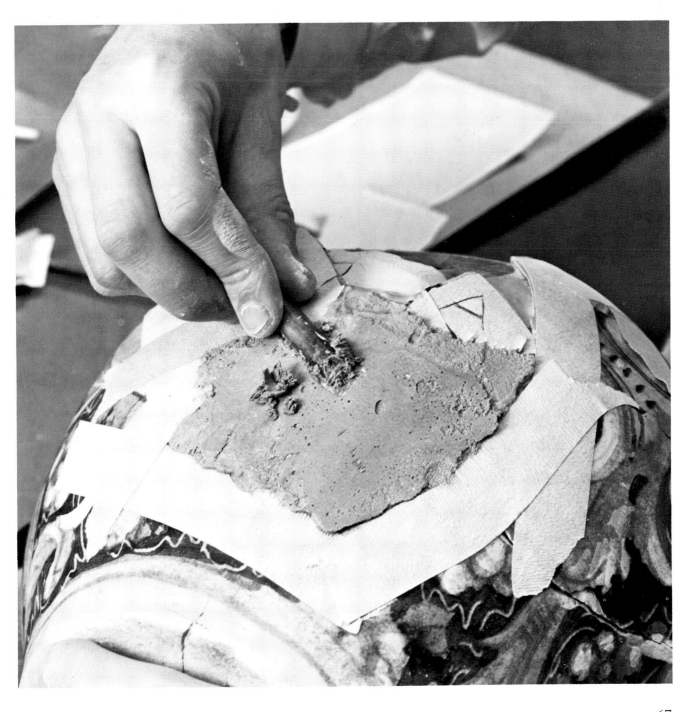

to use so hard a material unless one has a particular aptitude for slogging away with sandpaper and plenty of time to spend doing so. On a retouched piece of European faience there is a good chance that no one will know whether the support is made of plastic or not.

Given the extreme hardness of polyester, then, the restorer will be wise to take great pains over his shuttering and over the way he applies the fill, the idea being to have as little excess as possible to remove afterwards. He will also have protected the surrounding areas carefully, and when rubbing down the hardened fill with rasp, riffler, and sand-paper he will proceed very slowly. At the end, when he has to remove the protective surround of adhesive tape to get the surface of the filling down to the level of the glaze, he will be extra careful not to inflict any damage on the latter.

Any additives he has mixed with the polyester to tint it, thicken it, or give it the colour of the ware he is repairing will more or less seriously affect the rubbing-down process. If the polyester has been opacified with coloured pigments or whiting or if it is one of those ready-prepared polyesters used by monumental masons, the restorer will find himself blunting his rasps and rifflers in no time on the abrasive ingredients. It is best not to worry about

47
A Japanese Kakiemon vase. The neck is to be remade in polyester.

48
The polyester is applied to a cardboard support.

49
After polymerization the polyester neck is worked with the riffler.

50
The neck is now ready for retouching.

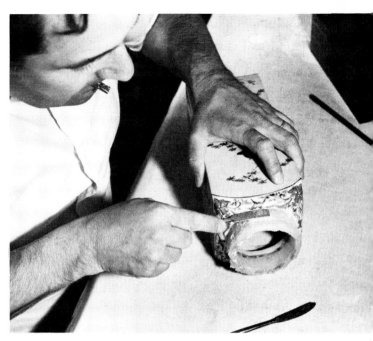

colour too much but to match for texture and let retouching do the rest. A polyester that is easy to work without excess wear on one's tools is one that has been thixotroped with silica and opacified with a suitable chemical whitener.

Shaping and rubbing-down once completed, there will be a certain number of corrections to be made – bubbles in the polyester, little bits missing, etc. These should be filled with fast-setting epoxy resin without worrying about the difference in colour (when it comes to retouching this can be eliminated by applying a ground); being fine and highly adhesive, epoxy resin will hold better than polyester in very small holes.

Polyester is not in fact particularly adhesive, and since it also shrinks slightly when it polymerizes the renewed fragment may come unstuck while being rubbed down, especially if it is not held on all sides by original material. The remedy is simple: glue it with epoxy resin and carry on rubbing down. Some restorers avert this possibility from the outset by applying a thin film of epoxy resin to the surrounding fractured edges before putting in the polyester; epoxy resin and polyester belong to different families, of course, but contact between them before polymerization appears to do no harm.

Other restorers drop polyester completely when renewing smaller fragments; they use fast-setting epoxy resin instead, which has the great advantage of remaining more flexible and workable than polyester, so that it can be shaped while setting. This is done with a spatula or a wet finger at a specific point in the polymerization process, and if it is done well there will only be a minimum of excess material to be removed afterwards.

Above a certain size of fragment, however, fast-setting epoxy resin may prove too flexible to match the rigidity of the ware concerned. What the restorer can do then – if the thickness of the ware allows – is to combine the advantages of the two types of plastic (the rigidity of polyester and the greater workability of fast-setting epoxy resin) by first applying polyester, bringing it up to within a millimetre or two of the surrounding surface, and then completing the missing fragment with fast-setting epoxy resin.

RENEWING FRAGMENTS ON PORCELAIN

There is porcelain and porcelain. As far as the restorer is concerned the thick and not very translucent porcelain of a Kakiemon vase from Japan will be treated in exactly the same way as a piece of glazed earthenware: the fragment will be renewed in polyester or fast-setting epoxy resin and the restorer will concentrate on texture rather than on colour. But when he is repairing a delicate Empire cup or a Sèvres or Meissen plate he may find it to his advantage to concentrate on achieving the same degree of translucency as the porcelain with a thixotropic polyester made opaline by the addition of a white colouring agent. Subsequent retouching of a large area will be greatly facilitated if the fill is translucent. Certain museographical restorations may even be left visible; like this they will be infinitely less offensive than if the fragment had been renewed in stucco.

The restorer, however, may think twice before using a translucent fill to renew a fragment of porcelain

51
The completed restoration.

that will subsequently be retouched: it may not be worth the trouble. But he will have no hesitation when it is a question of replacing decorative elements, such as the string of pearls on certain Louis XVI porcelains or a lion's head on a large piece from China – and even less when it comes to replacing a hand or other member on a Sèvres biscuit porcelain figurine that, having no glaze, can be left unretouched if the restorer manages to hit on exactly the right proportions of polyester and colouring agent.

It is extremely difficult to achieve a flawless surface with polyester and the restorer will find himself repeatedly making up a fresh batch of polyester to correct small imperfections. For this reason it is a good idea to tint a large quantity of polyester to the right shade of translucency, mixing it with its catalysts only as and when it is needed.

Renewing missing elements

Whatever type of ware he is dealing with the restorer may find himself having to renew or replace something other than a fragment of the shell – a handle on a Greek vase, for example, or a cherub on a Nevers faience, or a rose on the lid of a piece of Dresden china. This calls for certain specialized techniques.

In fact the problem is simpler than it appears. It is a question of renewing elements that, while contributing a great deal to the balance of the whole, do not form as integral a part of the object as, say, a fragment of its shell. It is extremely difficult to make a renewed fragment pass unobserved as regards texture and colour; it is very much less difficult to get away with a flower on a lid, which is stuck on anyway, or a new stucco handle on a Greek vase. The point where the fake meets the genuine is pretty small; the frontier between them is too inconspicuous to catch the eye and, in doing so, invite comparison. On the other hand the usually intricate detail on this type of excrescence – rose petals, shadows, spots – will delude the observer into thinking that it is an authentic part of the original. If the element is well made, retouching too will be very much less problematical than in the case of a fragment of a perfectly smooth surface.

SOFT EARTHENWARE – ARCHAEOLOGICAL FINDS
The element is roughly modelled in stucco tinted to the colour of the earthenware and finished off and rubbed down when dry.

It is essential to provide some reinforcement embedded in both the original piece and the stucco element. The restorer makes a hole in the earthenware in the middle of the place from which the element is missing (e.g. the root of a handle or knob); the diameter of the hole should be a quarter of that of the root and its depth three or four times its diameter. In soft earthenware this can be done easily with a metal drill, but as soon as the ware is fired a little harder the restorer may find himself resharpening his drill bit several times. Tungsten bits are best, though they only go down to three millimetres,

52
Renewing the handle of a black-figure vase in tinted plaster. A modelling-clay support holds the plaster in place.

which may be too much for very small jobs. Dentists' diamond drills will get through even the hardest ware.

A brass rod of the requisite size and shape is heated in a flame until red-hot and then cooled slowly. The restorer will previously have nicked it in various places with a file, metal saw, or grinding wheel to offer a good purchase to the stucco (cf. the iron rods used for reinforcing concrete, which are deliberately allowed to rust). He then beds the rod in the hole or holes (the rod to support a handle will be fixed at both ends) with epoxy resin adhesive.

Waiting until his tinted stucco has begun to thicken,

53
A flexible mould has been made from the model. Here a copy is being removed from the mould.

54
This lion's head is made of epoxy resin.

the restorer applies it to this support. Adhesive tape or modelling clay can be used to hold it in position while it sets.

Not until the stucco is completely dry does the restorer start rubbing it down with riffler, rat-tail file, and finally with little rolls of sandpaper. During the rubbing-down process one often finds one has to add more stucco here and there, in which case the only thing to remember is to wet the dry stucco well before putting fresh stucco on top of it.

The final stage, when the restorer has finished carving the replacement in the spirit of the original, is to harden it with a coat of clear shellac varnish.

GLAZED EARTHENWARE AND PORCELAIN

Simple elements missing from glazed earthenware, faience, and porcelain pieces can be replaced in the same manner except that the holes will need to be bored with a dentist's drill (or sent out to a specialist for drilling) and tinted; thixotropic polyester will take the place of stucco. This will be worked on the object after polymerizing on the same brass support.

In many cases the missing element may be extremely difficult to fashion by hand. It may be a complicated piece of sculpture like a rose or a bunch of flowers on the lid of a piece of Dresden china or the intricate handle of a Moustiers pitcher. If the restorer has nothing to go by but a photograph he will have no alternative but to proceed by hand, working his polyester replacement as best as he can with the appropriate tools – files, gravers, little ivory-carvers' gouges, dentists' drills, rifflers, etc.

CASTING

Very often, though, particularly in an old-established restorer's workshop, there will be an actual model to hand (ills. 53 and 54). The piece to be repaired may have an undamaged twin, or a number of Meissen figurines may have come in for repair at the same time, one with a hand missing; the restorer may not feel up to making a new hand himself, and he may find one on another figure that would do. In such cases he will proceed to take a casting, using a silicone elastomer as marketed by the major chemical industries or obtainable through an artists' materials dealer.

A silicone elastomer makes a flexible mould that does not need perfect clearance in order to deliver the model or the reproduction; containing its own

55
This vase had lost its lid. The restorer is reproducing the decoration on a porcelain lid that will then be glazed.

stripping agent, it will give an absolutely faithful reproduction even down to the mat or gloss surface of the original.

It comes in the form of a cream (there is also a thixotropic elastomer) that polymerizes with the aid of a catalyst supplied with it, and it is applied in two stages. Having built a wall of modelling clay round the element of which he wants to take a casting, the restorer puts on an initial coat of elastomer with a brush in order to avoid the possibility of air bubbles getting trapped inside the mould; he then pours the rest over the model, filling the basin he has formed with modelling clay.

Twenty-four hours later polymerization will be

complete and the mould can usually be drawn off like a glove, though if the model presents major clearance problems the elastomer may have to be cut with a razor blade to make it deliver more easily. Once one has developed a certain facility with elastomers one may be able to take castings of quite complicated objects.

For the reproduction it is better to use slow-setting epoxy resin than polyester; contact with the elastomer will usually interfere with the setting of polyester, which will consequently not give very faithful castings. A film of tinted epoxy resin is first brushed into the mould; this is then filled, and the setting of the epoxy resin can be speeded up by placing the mould in a very low oven. If the reproduction turns out too pliable, as epoxy resin has a tendency to do, particularly in small volumes, it can be stiffened by inserting small brass or steel rods before the epoxy resin sets.

The reconstituted element is then fixed to the original with the aid of a dowel pin and epoxy resin adhesive. Fresh material is added or excess material removed as required, and retouching does the rest. Casting can be an extremely useful technique, enabling the restorer to turn out any number of handles for precious porcelain teacups, bunches of flowers to go on lids, heads, hands, or whatever it

may be. It is not often that he will fail to find the ideal model.

RENEWING FRAGMENTS AND ELEMENTS WITH CERAMIC WARE

Taking apart old restoration jobs one sometimes comes across a fragment of glazed earthenware or porcelain – it may be a triangle measuring several centimetres – that has been replaced in the identical ware and fired together with the retouched decoration. This would be the finest restoration method of all if nine times out of ten the restorer had not been obliged to repaint the entire piece, neither the shape nor the colour of the renewed portion being perfect. Usually this method is applied only to more or less excrescent elements – handles, feet, necks, knobs, and so on.

It is best used in renewing – in glazed earthenware, stoneware, or porcelain – completely independent elements such as lids (ill. 55) or complete pieces missing from some kind of arrangement. For example one of those Chinese sweetmeat dishes consisting of a number of small recipients of various shapes that together make up a lotus flower might have one piece missing. A good porcelain manufacturer will be able to make and glaze a pretty faithful modern replacement.

IV RETOUCHING

We have completed part of the restoration process, but the piece is hardly presentable as yet, its shape and decoration being obscured by various patches of fill. We now come to the operation that possibly constitutes the restorer's trade proper – retouching, which means making the filling match the original ware around it. I say "match" rather than "blend with" because not all retouching aims at being invisible; the restorer may adopt other solutions, combining museographical honesty with elegance to marry a restored and still visible portion with the adjacent original.

The purpose of retouching being to camouflage a repair in such a way that the eye travels over it without being arrested, it stands to reason that it will be virtually impossible to achieve this marriage between the filling and the ware around it without painting over a certain amount of that ware as well. One simple way of tackling a difficult retouching job would be to repaint the entire piece, but though this would conceal the fractures it is more than likely that the colours would bear little resemblance to the Nevers or Rouen originals.

In fact, as we shall see, the best retouching job is one that extends as little as possible beyond the confines of the filled area. The closer the restorer's palette is to the original, the less need there will be for him to "fade out" on the surrounding original. The ideal – the impossible ideal – is to render the repair invisible by retouching it alone. Impossible, that is, if the restorer is after complete invisibility; if he is not concerned to deceive the eye but is satisfied with the goal "visible from close up, invisible from a distance" he will be able, on certain types of ware, given optimal colour matching, to confine his retouching strictly to the surface of the fill.

Colours

To the uninitiated, artists' colours are always either a paste or a liquid – oil paint, gouache, or watercolour – that can be applied to a support. What is not generally appreciated is that all three in fact contain the identical powder. It is merely mixed with a different medium in each case; a different adhesive is used to glue the grains of colour together.

This gives the restorer a wide choice. He can mix up his colours or pigments as he calls them with more or less anything he likes – from high-gloss varnishes to produce a brilliant finish to adhesives of various strengths to give various degrees of mat finish.

As a rule the restorer will have two boxes of pigments. The first, with some ten compartments only, contains the colours that enable him to imitate what might be called "natural" colours – the colour of mat earthenware, the colour of the chalk deposits that form on antique wares, the colour of stone, of rust, the reds and blacks of Greek vases. He calls them "earths," and that is what they are – finely pulverized earths. Different types of soil produce yellow ochres, umbers, raw siennas. Burnt, these earths produce other colours: burnt umber, burnt sienna. The first box will also contain a black and a cobalt blue – the latter being used not for mixing with red ochre to make purple but for taking the edge off a colour that is too sharp. For example, to match the shade of a pinkish-beige terracotta by Clodion or a piece of neolithic ware the restorer will need to mix exactly the right quantities of three pigments: red ochre, yellow ochre, and raw umber. In all probability he will then need a dash of cobalt blue to "break" the resultant shade and a certain amount of whiting to lighten it. Experience will show that imitating natural colours does not often call for the use of burnt pigments. The beginner will tend to use the whole gamut at his disposal, possibly including rarer pigments such as Kassel earth, or even sepia. The best advice anyone can give him is that he should try the three pigments mentioned above first; it is very rarely that more will be needed. If the ware to be matched has a greenish tinge it may be necessary to add a little emerald green, but even here yellow ochre and cobalt blue will between them usually cover the case.

This first box needs no special care; a little dust, even a few grains of pigment in the wrong compartment are nothing to worry about. The second box, however, the one used for retouching glazed earthenware and porcelain, needs to be looked after very carefully indeed.

The job of the second box will be to imitate all the colours that the chemistry of slip-painting has come up with at various stages of every civilization. Earths will be inadequate to retouch a Chinese oxblood glaze, an Iznik plate, or a Sèvres turquoise. This box will contain the so-called "fine" colours, various metal oxides in the brightest possible tints. (Restorers complain that pigments are not as luminous as they used to be. Ultramarine and carmine used to match a Nevers blue; nowadays it is difficult to get anything but a dull shade out of them, and it is next to impossible to match a really good Sèvres turquoise with the drab cerulean blues on the market today.) If the earths and whiting of the first box offer as it were the notes of the chord, the metal oxides of the second box provide the chromatic scale.

What happens when a restorer sets about matching a colour?

Well, it is in fact not unlike tuning a musical instrument, where it is a question of making a string

56–59
An old repair of an incomplete Italian plate.

56
Detail showing the perfection of a large repair in restoring varnish. Unfortunately it has crackled with age.

82

vibrate with the same number of vibrations as a standard string. But whereas a good ear can hear the tiniest interval and always distinguish a minor note from a major one, the eye is incapable of, for example, distinguishing a green made up of yellow and blue from a green with a single wavelength. The

57
The plate as it looks to the naked eye.

58
X-ray photography reveals in black the part that was remade in stucco.

59
Comparison of ultra-violet and X-ray photographs shows how the retouching overlaps onto the original portion. The light parts are repainted; the flaking of this old repair reveals the original decoration.

restorer's approach to colour matching is thus an empirical one; he must try to reproduce the most subtle shades with a certain limited number of pigments, never using more than three at a time (plus white) if he does not want to sacrifice all luminosity. He must practise analysing colours until he can tell almost instinctively that this particular blue, for instance, needs a little red in it, or that a particular shade of ivory can only be achieved by adding a dash of lemon yellow to give an edge to what looked at first sight like a straightforward pale pinkish beige. Very often a colour will baffle one, so strong is the tendency to see what one knows rather than what one sees. The restorer must be an impressionist here, innocent of all preconceptions, open to the astonishing amount of carmine that may be present in a simple blue.

All this is extremely difficult to formulate theoretically, and until someone invents an electronic pigment doser to do the job for him the restorer will have to continue to operate almost at the level of the subconscious, his palette knife reaching out automatically for a little bit of one pigment here, a little bit of another pigment there, as he works his way by trial and error towards exactly the right shade — without being able to say afterwards quite how he got there. With no prescription to go on, the mind is thrown back on intuition, and it is no exaggeration to say that a difficult piece of retouching calls for a very high degree of concentration indeed.

Whites

Before we go any further we must say something about a colour that, pursuing the musical analogy, can be compared to the mute on a musical instrument, or to the force with which a note is struck.

The restorer will use three kinds of white: whiting, titanium dioxide, and a third that consists in the absence of any other colour.

Let us start with this mysterious white that does not exist — and yet is the most important and the most widely-used of the three. Think of the watercolourist. He never paints in white; his white is his paper. If he wants to lighten a blue he simply lets more of

the support show through, and if he wants a pure white he leaves the paper blank. Here we touch on one of the most delicate refinements of restoration and retouching work, namely transparency. The restorer often needs to be awake to the fact that a particular green, for example, can only be achieved by laying a transparent blue over a yellow ground. As often as not it will be a question of preparing a very pure shade and then dirtying it by painting over it in such a way that it shows through. The process is called scumbling, and it is one of the keys to successful restoration.

Another widely-used white, employed almost exclusively to produce mat shades in conjunction with earth pigments, is ordinary whiting as sold by paint merchants and as used in the last chapter for filling. To understand its use it is essential to make the experiment of wetting a small quantity and applying it to a sheet of dark paper. As the experiment will show, it does not really become visible until dry. In the wet state it will have little effect on the coloured pigment it is intended to lighten, and the restorer is obliged to guess what that effect will be when the paint is dry. Gloss varnishes are no good with it; mixed with a very light binding agent, it is the white restorers use for lightening all their mat natural tones. It offers limitless possibilities, as experience will show. Allowing various transparent effects, it can be used to cloud a colour that is too sharp or, applied as a really light scumble, make it vibrate with the most subtle nuances.

Titanium dioxide, on the other hand, is used in conjunction with bright colours. It is extremely white and holds its opacity and consequently its full value in the glossiest varnishes. It lightens a colour directly and the resultant shade will not change in

60
Retouching a piece of Moustiers faience. The restorer is working carefully towards the correct white for the ground. Also visible in the photograph are the ground-glass palette, knife, coloured pigments, glass muller, and sable-hair brushes.

drying. It is useful for imitating the shiny glaze on glazed earthenware and porcelain, and it can be used on its own for retouching white porcelain. The restorer will gain an appreciation of its potential in applying it to particular cases.

Mediums

The purpose of the medium is to make the tiny grains of powdered pigment adhere to one another and to the object being retouched. As honey and gum arabic are the medium of watercolour and ox-gall the medium of certain types of gouache, the mediums of pottery restoration are various varnishes and adhesives. The choice of medium will depend on the degree of gloss required in the finish. Polyvinyl adhesive will give a thick, mat paint; a light rubber varnish can be used for anything from a satiny gloss to a dead mat finish; picture varnish and acrylic varnish will imitate a brilliant glaze.

Attempts are currently being made to find a gloss varnish that will not yellow with age (ill. 61). As every restorer knows, restoration jobs on white porcelain have the annoying habit of looking perfect for two or three years and then starting to go yellow, revealing the extent of the repair. What happens is that the lac molecules in the varnish oxidize, and the ideal thing would be to find a type of molecule that was already saturated with oxygen. Acrylic varnish does not yellow, but it is very much less strong and less fine than traditional lacquers. Recent research has come up with various polyurethane varnishes; these are extremely strong and do not yellow, but they are rather difficult to use.

Mat retouching

FOR MUSEOGRAPHICAL PURPOSES
If the restorer is not out to conceal the fact that a piece of pottery has been mended, there is all the more reason for his adopting a solution that is particularly elegant.

I use the word "elegant" deliberately since it seems to me highly appropriate here. A gesture – be it a present given or a service rendered – is judged elegant not in terms of size but as evincing discretion. A kindly remark need not take the form of an extended panegyric; what is required is the right word in the circumstances. It is the same with a good job of retouching, which should be simple and restrained, not thick with overpaint and confused with second thoughts. And visible retouching, if it is well done, is the most elegant kind of all.

Take for example an ancient piece of earthenware, fired at a very low temperature; a number of fragments have been renewed in tinted plaster. One solution would be to do no retouching at all. Very often, if the piece is of purely archaeological interest, the restorer need do no more than renew the missing fragments with plaster tinted to match the general colour of the body as closely as possible. I would not suggest he goes as far as certain American restorers, who make their fillings systematically with plaster tinted a uniform shade of grey – an honest but far from elegant solution that runs counter to the whole idea of retouching.

61
Detail of an Italian plate.
An old repair using restoring varnish has yellowed considerably so that it has become extremely evident.

62
Sarcophagus. South India.
On a purely archaeological subject such as this, visible repairs are admissible. Musée Guimet, Paris.

63
A light glaze will bring the filled portions up to the exact shade of the ware. Only the black figures will be retouched, and these only on the repaired portion.

If a filling has been made to the exact colour of the body and the ware carries a decoration, the restorer can proceed in a variety of ways while still leaving his retouching visible (ill. 62). For example he can just sketch in the outline of the decoration to allow the eye to appreciate its continuity and the roundness of the surface. Or he can adopt a bolder approach that, if successful, constitutes the acme of museographical restoration. This is the solution so excellently represented by the Cretan ceramics in

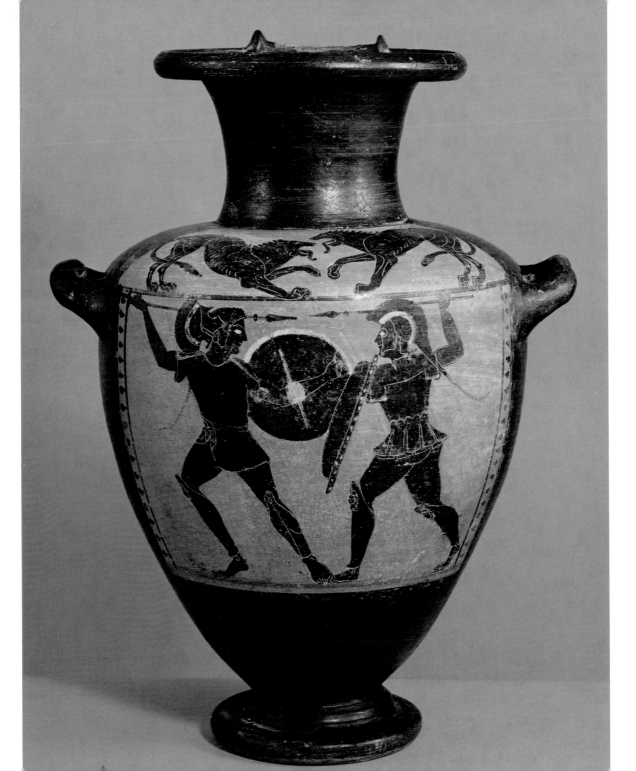

the museum at Iraklion on which the decoration has been reconstituted in its entirety in the same colour but a shade or two lighter, with the retouching encroaching at no point on the original. This type of restoration constitutes something in the nature of an archaeological thesis. At Iraklion sometimes up to seventy-five percent of the piece is missing. The surviving decoration makes no sense to the un-initiated, so what the archaeologist-restorer has done is to advance a proposition; honesty is sat-isfied because the restored portions are lighter and can be redone at any time.

The first step is to varnish the filling to make it properly waterproof. This is done with clear shellac varnish in a generous proportion of alcohol, using a fine brush. Since this will have the effect of bringing up the colour of the filling slightly, if the restorer means to do no retouching he will have taken the precaution of tinting his fill a shade too light. For the purposes of archaeological study the match need not be exact, but if the restorer feels he is too far off target, or if the piece is decorated and he wants to continue the decoration on the filled portion, he will go on to retouch.

A water-based medium is best for mat earthenware. The restorer will place on a frosted glass palette quantities of the few earth pigments needed to reproduce the earthenware range of colours, adding a sizeable heap of whiting, a small heap of cobalt blue, and a few drops of polyvinyl adhesive. He will also have a hair-dryer handy; this is indispensable for quick colour checks, since the colours will tend to lighten as they dry in proportion to the amount of whiting they contain. He will prepare his colour by mixing carefully together adhesive, pigments, and whiting. The amount of adhesive needed is something only experience can tell him. Too much will give a transparent, semi-gloss effect that will not cover well; too little, and the paint will fail to adhere to the body.

The paint is applied with a fine brush, the size of the latter depending on the area to be covered (ill. 63). When retouching filled-in cracks it is important to try and keep strictly to the filling, though this is sometimes difficult. If the filling has been rubbed down to the exact level of the surrounding ware it is important to apply the paint as thinly as it will still cover; in some cases the restorer will use a very fine sandpaper to remove the brush marks. This done, he may still find himself some way from the glossy finish of the ware he is trying to match. Dry rubbing with a cake of clear wax will add a very gentle lustre, or a similar effect can be obtained by spray-ing or brushing on a delicate scumble in a slightly darker tone, using a liquor prepared, for example, with raw umber, a drop of shellac varnish, and a large proportion of alcohol. It will of course be necessary to have allowed for these processes by making the initial colour a shade too light. For the purposes of visible retouching they can be done at any stage.

Any decoration will also have to be done with this kind of transparent scumble. The scanty decoration found on primitive wares — often consisting of parallel lines — is done in very fine, very mat glazes. The restorer will use a liquor based on polyvinyl acetate adhesive or shellac varnish, choosing and handling his brush in such a way as to reproduce the

Retouching is confined strictly to the filled portions and the repair, though it can be seen close up, is invisible at a distance.

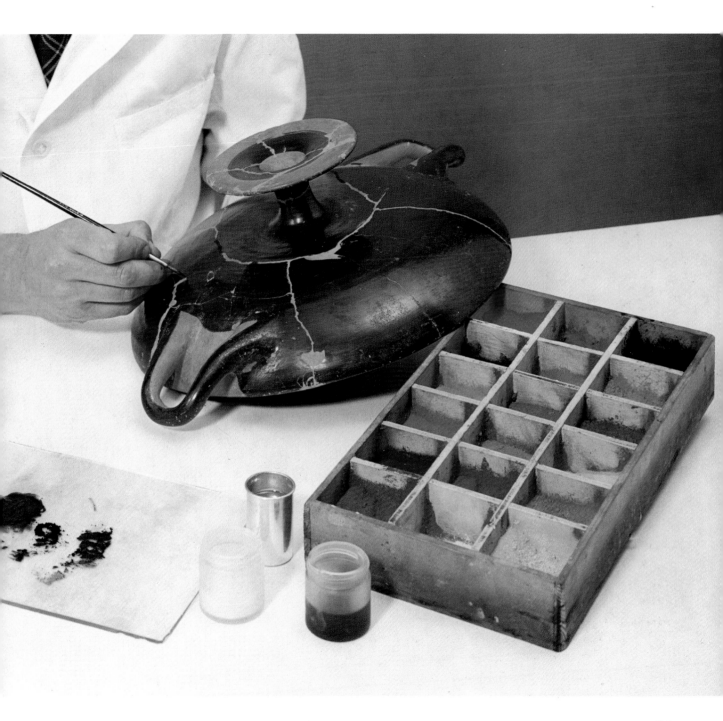

different thicknesses and consequently the different degrees of transparency of the original glaze. A light wax rub will give the right kind of gentle gleam. A special word is necessary as regards retouching really high-quality black-figure and red-figure pottery. The walls of these wares are thin, the black glaze has a semi-gloss finish with a metallic sheen that is extremely difficult to copy, and on the finest examples this black glaze is distributed very evenly over an absolutely smooth surface with, at most, very faint turning marks – which only make copying even more difficult.

Large numbers of Greek wares have been restored and in many cases the restorer attempted to camouflage the fractures. Finding the metallic black glaze impossible to imitate, however, he tended to end up by covering all the original glaze on the figures. On the other hand he tended to give the portions left red the same gloss as the black figures. Much of the charm of these wares lies in the contrast between the semi-gloss of the black glaze with its metallic sheen and the mat quality of the portions left red and the purple and white highlights – not to mention the pure and virile style of the figures, nothing of which survives such wholesale retouching.

The restorer is best advised not to attempt an invisible restoration on this type of ware but to direct all his talents towards achieving a perfect alliance of honesty and elegance. Needless to say his gluing and filling must be flawless. The fillings, once varnished, must exactly match the colour of the earthenware, i.e. the portions left red on black-figure wares. They must also be perfectly flush, with any little scratches left by the abrasive running in the direction of the turning marks. The ideal is to make further retouching superfluous on the red portions.

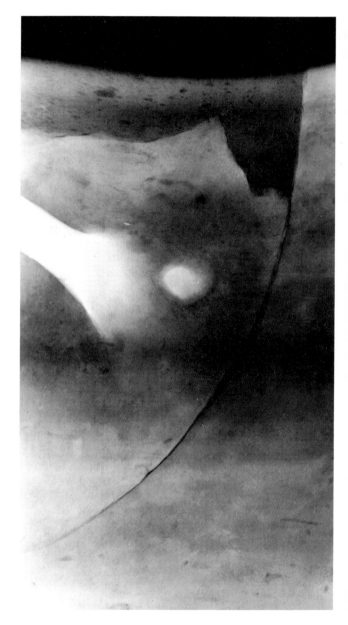

64/65
An invisible repair to a piece of Mycenaean pottery. The X-ray photograph shows the missing portion. Note the effects of material on the restored edge.

93

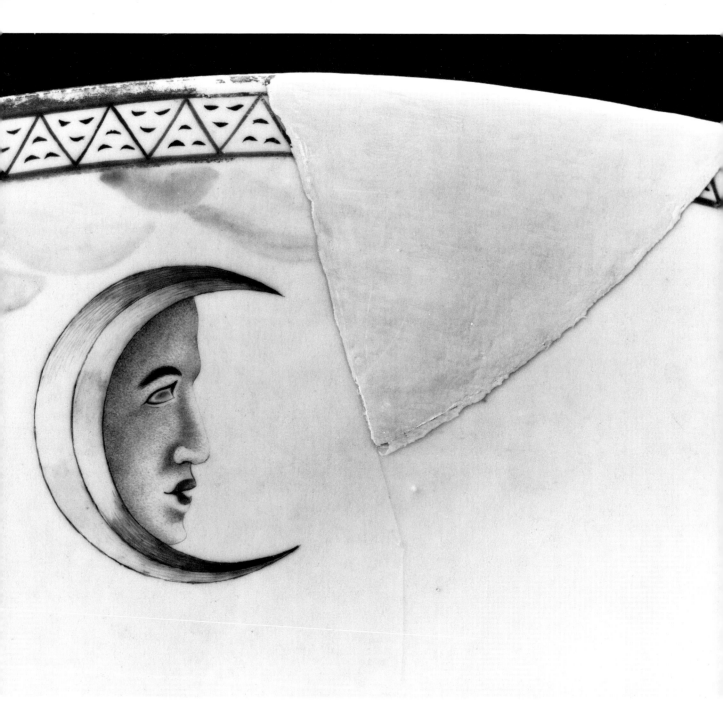

The next stage is to capture the metallic black by means of the right doses of powdered plumbago, ivory black, and sometimes other pigments such as ultramarine and emerald green. Where the sheen is particularly pronounced a little silver powder can be added (but only a little, because it goes a long way). My favourite medium here is water-soluble polyvinyl adhesive; it dries to a highly mat finish that, if rubbed down with a very fine sandpaper, can be brought up to the gloss of the original with virgin wax or, if that is not enough, with shellac varnish. Polyvinyl acetate is a rather tricky medium to use, however, forming a fairly thick paint that tends to hold a lot of brush marks, which necessitates careful rubbing-down. If the restorer is not entirely comfortable with it as a medium he can use a clear shellac varnish (I would definitely advise against restoring varnish or turpentine picture varnish). Once one has captured the exact shade the great secret is to apply the paint without overlapping the original, though another problem is that some of these metallic blacks have a suggestion of red in them. In all but a few exceptional cases this is due to the black glaze being transparent and the earthenware body showing through. To reproduce this effect the restorer must give his paint the same transparency and apply it very thinly.

This method is above all useful for retouching fairly large fillings and renewed fragments. For making good the tiny chips that always occur along cracks it is often better to colour-match one's fill with plumbago and black pigment, using a rubber varnish. Once dry, the fill is rubbed down to reveal the lips of each hole and then waxed to give it the requisite gloss. This type of fill can only be used for very small holes, however; used in larger quantities, it will tend to crack.

INVISIBLE MAT RETOUCHING

It may sometimes be possible and advantageous to retouch a piece of unglazed or very lightly glazed earthenware invisibly (ills. 64 and 65).

Think of a rhython, for example, one of those zoomorphic drinking vessels, or a Tanagra figurine. For one thing the interest of the piece lies not in its surface decoration but in its shape, and for another a thick, mat slip, the presence of irregularities, and a varied patina make invisible retouching both feasible and desirable.

The essence of invisible retouching, whether in mat or gloss, consists in achieving an imperceptible transfer from the painted area to the original surface. The secret is gradually to apply less and less paint until each colour "fades out" a little way beyond the fracture.

How is this done in the case of a mat finish?

Again it is a question of analysing the quality of the surface matter and the different layers that make it up. On a Tanagra or Myrina terracotta, for example, we find a slightly grainy, orange-coloured body covered with a thin eggshell slip that is flaking off; part of this is in turn covered by coarse chalk deposits. On this type of surface it is undoubtedly easier to camouflage one's repair completely than to do an elegant piece of visible retouching. There is of course an enormous variety of textures and finishes

66
Museum repair to a piece of East India Company porcelain. The value of the piece is documentary. The restorer felt no necessity to make an invisible repair, which would have involved repainting a very much larger portion.

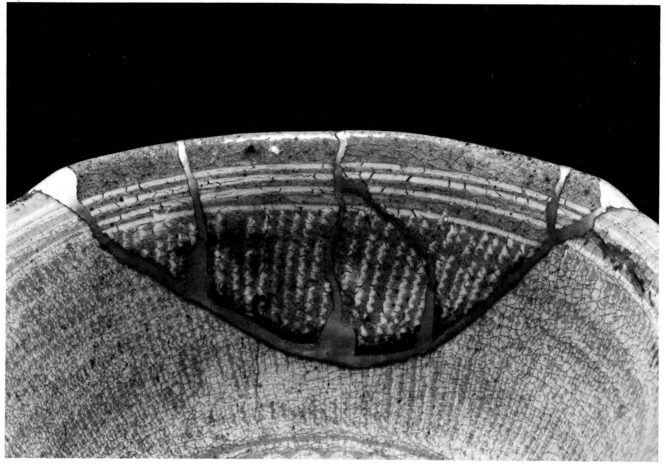

67
Korean bowl. A reconstituted fragment or a fragment of another bowl cut to fit with a gold-lacquer fillet (see p. 15). Musée Guimet, Paris.

68
Good gluing and some slight filling in the general colour of the piece are sometimes all that is necessary.

in antique pottery and at this level retouching is going to be based largely on intuition, inventiveness, and adaptation to a different situation in each case. But we can give a few general principles.

For example a patch – i.e. a filling or a renewed fragment – is always easier to conceal than a line. The eye will invariably follow a line through unless it has been retouched perfectly. So one of the restorer's tricks is to break a line up by means of artificial irregularities – provided, of course, that these are a feature of the surface concerned.

Taking our Tanagra terracotta, then, the first step is to make the fill slightly lighter than the colour of the

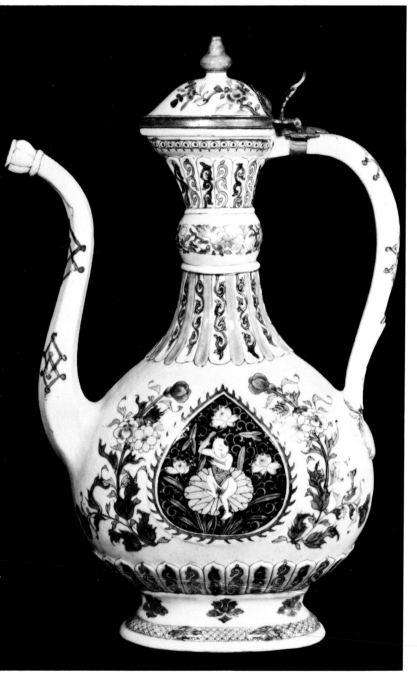

body; the filling is lightly varnished, and an poly-vinyl-based paint in the exact colour of the body is then fitched rather than brushed on (i.e. using a brush of polecat hair applied at right angles to the surface). A little more than the area of the filling is painted in this way, with the paint layer getting thinner and thinner towards the edge. Polyvinyl adhesive has the advantage of deteriorating in water but not dissolving immediately, so that polyvinyl-based paint mixtures can be painted one on top of another with no problems.

The white slip can be added where required with the aid of a spatula. It will be based on a lightly tinted whiting paste and a very small quantity of adhesive so that it can be very simply "flaked" by applying adhesive tape to it and then ripping this off to reproduce the random flaking of the original slip. It will be gently rubbed down, soiled and patinated with a very light watercolour scumble, and finally sealed and consolidated with a thin coat of varnish. (A well-distributed soiling effect can be achieved by cropping an ordinary paintbrush and using it to spatter on tiny drops of paint or larger splashes.)

The chalk deposit can be imitated by fitching on a thick tinted adhesive paste or by removing some of the original deposit from a less visible place, mixing it with a little adhesive, and applying it to the retouched area.

69
Chinese pitcher. *Famille rose*. Musée Guimet, Paris.

70
A pitcher of the same type that has been turned into a flask after damage and the addition of a Dutch fitting made of gilded bronze.

I outline this treatment of a particular case simply as an exemple of the infinite number of different surfaces that can occur. Imitating them poses a challenge to the restorer's inventiveness and capacity to adapt to different situations while still observing a certain number of general principles.

Visible gloss retouching

A more difficult task is gloss retouching in bright colours or pure white on glazed earthenware, stoneware, and porcelain.

Certain cases call for visible retouching. For example the restorer may have done his gluing so well that the labour and difficulty of retouching for invisibility – together with the risk of its yellowing with age – would be out of all proportion to the minor unsightliness of a certain number of hair lines on the surface of the piece.

For museographical purposes, too, when a damaged piece of glazed earthenware or porcelain is chiefly of documentary interest as an example of the work of a particular factory, visible retouching is preferable (ill. 66). Or a piece may be so badly broken and its glaze so difficult to imitate that it would be impossible to camouflage the repair without re-painting the whole thing. In tackling a turquoise Persian bowl from Rhagae with its finely crackled glaze and delicate rainbow effects, the restorer will do best to confine himself to filling in the colour of the body – generally eggshell – and retouching in turquoise on the filled portions alone. In each case the restorer will mix and apply his colour according to more or less the same method as for the invisible retouching described below.

Another kind of visible retouching is in fact a supremely refined form of anti-matching, as it were. I refer to the gold-lacquer restoration work found on certain Japanese and sometimes Korean tea-ceremony wares (ill. 67). This type of repair is well in tune with the Japanese idea of beauty, which is often based on a contrast between simplicity and refinement, and understanding it involves a close study of these tea-ceremony wares with their distorted shapes induced by over-firing and their thick, irregular, clumsy glazes that in reality conceal a tremendous wealth of colour and a sophisticated knowledge of ceramic technique. We often find, topping an irregularly-rounded, deliberately heavy pot, a tiny ivory lid that is superbly turned and polished – refinement contrasted with simplicity. The pot has cracked on the stove, say, or has broken as a result of being dropped. There is no question of trying to imitate the immensely thick glaze; for one thing it would be extremely difficult to do so and for another it would be diametrically opposed to the Japanese way of thinking. No, the restorer positively takes advantage of the accident to make the piece even more beautiful than before, encircling each crack, each chip out of the glaze with a ribbon of gold laquer. In the Guimet Museum in Paris you can see a large Korean bottle that sags slightly at the centre as a result of being fired too hot. The glaze – an inimitable shade of white – is extremely thick and in places has been refused by the stoneware body; these patches with no glaze have been filled with gold lacquer. Two missing patches at the neck have been filled, one with gold lacquer and the other with black lacquer on which the artist has painted a tiny bouquet of gold foliage that contrasts sharply with the contrived rusticity of the whole. This refinement of the art of restoration almost became a vice when people deliberately broke things in order to be able to cover them with a delicate golden network.

The method is comparable to that used by Europeans in mending certain types of Chinese porcelain vessel with the aid of a neat gilded bronze or silver fitting; the foot of a vase became a lid, for example, with the addition of a bronze adaptor; or a pitcher like the one illustrated – but broken – was turned into a flask with a charming stopper of gilded and engraved copper (ills. 69 and 70).

Invisible gloss retouching on glazed earthenware and porcelain

It may be a mistake to deal with retouching on these two types of ware under the same heading, because if it is relatively easy to effect a perfect repair on an opaque glazed-earthenware body that does not call for numerous coats of varnish, trying to imitate the depth and transparency of porcelain with a colour opaque enough to conceal a filling belongs to what might be called the higher restoration, the summit of what *trompe l'œil* and scumbling can achieve. Apart from the degree of difficulty, however, the pigments, varnishes, and methods used are exactly the same.

You should hear a really great restorer of glazed earthenware and porcelain analysing a glaze. Where the layman sees only white he is capable of distin-

71
Once the ground is complete the decoration is redone in glaze.

72
Touching-up with the epoxy resin gun.

guishing three or four superimposed shades that result in the final colour of the glaze with all its subtleties and depths.

The glaze may be thinner on the raised portions, allowing the pinkish body to show through very faintly, in which case the restorer will treat the raised portions of his fillings with a pinkish wash

that will show through a second coat painted over it. A way of imitating the depth of porcelain is to allow a greyer coat to show through other, more milky coats. It takes a very keen eye indeed to analyse a glaze.

A further difficulty lies in making the transition from repair to original, from fake to authentic, invisible. This may not be too hard to achieve on a mat, opaque Tanagra figurine or even on a piece of glazed earthenware if the colours are bright and

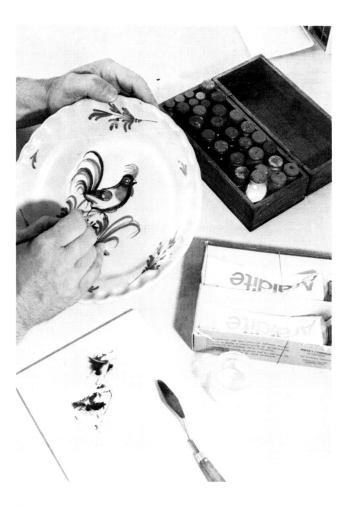

73
The decoration is completed with the brush.

74
The finished restoration.

shiny and the decoration full of variety, but it will be very much more difficult in the case of a translucent porcelain with no decoration and a flawless surface absolutely uniform in colour. Research is currently being done into ways of applying thinner and thinner films of varnish to achieve a perfectly invisible transition.

Traditional brush retouching

Pigments and titanium dioxide need to be ground extremely fine in their varnish medium to reconstitute the flawlessly smooth surface of a high-quality glaze. This is done with an ivory palette knife and a glass muller on a ground-glass palette.

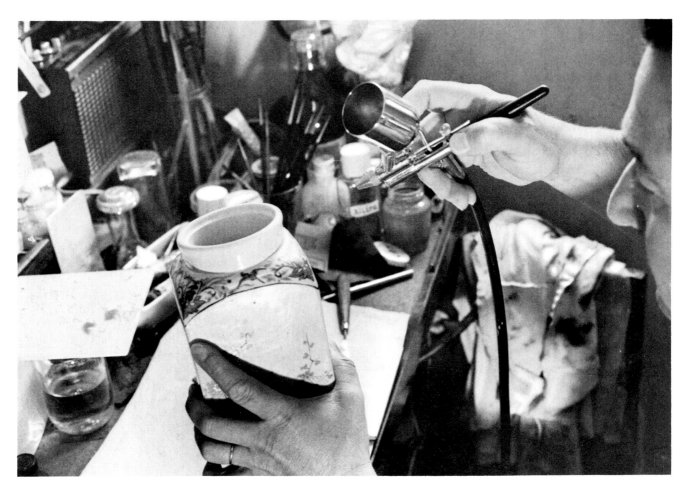

75/76
Japanese Kakiemon vase. The neck is finished. Retouching recreates the depth of the porcelain. The thickness of the glaze is felt in the decoration.

75
Several coats of tinted varnish sprayed one on top of another will reconstitute the ground exactly.

Having analysed the glaze he is dealing with, the restorer begins by reproducing the ground without worrying about the decoration at this stage. Two or three coats may be necessary, and if the first contains relatively little varnish, the last may consist of almost pure varnish.

The different coats are applied with a flat sable brush and are made to fade out on the original glaze slightly beyond the edge of the filling. Sometimes a good way of getting a thinner first coat is to apply the brush at right angles to the surface of the piece and "fitch" the varnish on. Each coat is left to dry and is then carefully rubbed down.

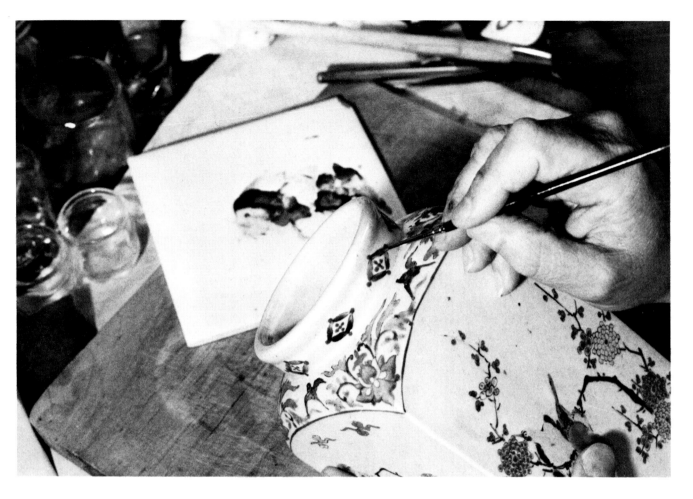

The ground is now ready for the decoration. If there is not too much of this missing — if, for example, the restorer is not called upon to reproduce half of a mythological scene on a piece of Italian majolica — retouching the decoration will soon prove a fairly simple affair and may even turn out to be the saving of a restorer who is not too sure of himself with regard to grounds. A variety of bright colours is easier to match than a particular shade of off-white, and a slight error is much less likely to show up. The

76
The decoration is reconstituted in epoxy resin.

problem of fading out does not arise if one is repainting a flower or a line, and it may sometimes be possible to extrapolate from the existing design a logical motif to cover up a repair; a crack may be camouflaged by extending the stalk of a flower, for example, or a chip or a pair of staple holes may be concealed by means of an invented motif. Provided

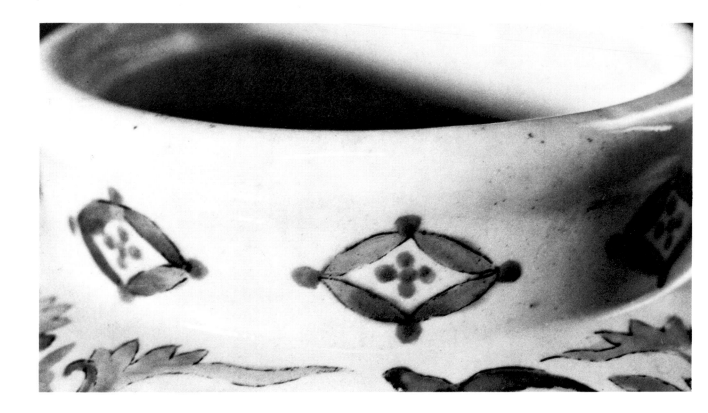

the invention is in keeping with the rest of the decoration this type of retouching will be completely invisible.

Retouching with a spray gun

There are disadvantages in applying varnish with a brush. For one thing the varnish tends to dry with the brush marks still in it, and for another it is extremely difficult to brush varnish on very thinly and fade out in the correct manner just beyond the edge of the filling. Also a fresh coat of varnish can have the effect of dissolving previous coats.

77
The neck of the Kakiemon vase has been retouched and is now finished.

For several years now restorers have been using a miniature compressed-air spray gun that allows them to spray polymerizable varnishes and achieve the most subtle scumbling effects (ills. 75–77).
Amazing results have been achieved on glazed earthenware and porcelain by spraying epoxy resin dissolved in trichlorethylene. Three or four coats are sprayed on, one after another, each coat being left to dry before the next is added. Some gentle rubbing-down is necessary between coats if an absolutely smooth finish is required, or on the con-

trary the epoxy resin can be allowed to polymerize in a series of droplets to imitate certain "orange-peel" glazes; a final spray of untinted epoxy resin is applied under a stream of warm air. Epoxy resin being impossible to repolish, the last coat is not rubbed down.

The decoration is brush retouched with epoxy resin and a greater or lesser quantity of trichlorethylene. Colouring epoxy resin calls for enormous experience since certain pigments undergo a change during polymerization. Oil colours in which the pigments are already insulated by a medium hold their colour in epoxy resin.

It is very easy to create the kind of thicknesses that are often a feature of pottery decoration – even the occasionnally very thick glazes that occur on modern wares.

But if epoxy resin is extremely convenient in that it allows one to imitate any kind of glaze, it has the serious disadvantage of yellowing with age. In fact it is passing steadily out of use, particularly for white grounds, and is being replaced by a polyurethane varnish that does not yellow – though neither does it reproduce so well the mellow effect of a glaze that has run slightly in the kiln. A successful marriage of the two techniques is to do the grounds, scumbles, transparencies, and final coats in polyurethane varnish while using epoxy resin for the coloured decoration. Polyurethane varnish has the further important advantage that it can be rubbed down and then repolished to give a really smooth surface. At this level of restoration anything goes; the restorer will feel free to try any invention, any trick that will help him to reproduce a glaze he may never have come across before. Certain Japanese porcelain wares, for example, have tiny black specks in the body that show through the glaze – an effect the restorer can reproduce by incorporating a few grains from a sheet of sand paper in his first coat of polyurethane varnish. The flaws in certain glazes can be imitated by spraying a fine mist of water onto the freshly-applied varnish. The metallic glaze on a Hispano-Moorish plate can be reconstituted by adding a little powdered bronze to the epoxy resin or the polyurethane varnish.

But here we are getting into the kind of *haute cuisine* where the recipes are difficult to formulate exactly. This is the domain of the gifted restorer, and each will have his own way of exploiting to the full the new materials that are constantly becoming available.

V GLASS

As far as its restoration is concerned, glass can be looked upon as being the most difficult type of pottery to repair. Like pottery, it is used to make vessels that have a tendency to break, but with glass the walls of the vessel are sometimes so thin as to make gluing problematical, and the fact that they are transparent makes camouflaging the repair, already difficult enough on translucent porcelain, frankly impossible.

Gluing modern glass

The restorer (though not the chemist) will group under this heading, as opposed to antique glass, which is devitrified and iridescent, all completely transparent materials such as glass itself, crystal, and even rock crystal, all of which present exactly the same problems.

They can never be glued invisibly. One might think that a perfectly transparent adhesive, as clear as the glass itself, provided that it contained no bubbles and completely filled the space between two fragments, could be totally invisible. Not so, alas, for the simple reason that glass and adhesive have different indices of refraction. The restorer would need to find an adhesive with the same index of refraction as glass. But then he would need another one for crystal, which has a different index again, to say nothing of the infinite variety of types of glass composition.

Cyanocrylates have an index of refraction very close to that of glass and are a good type of adhesive to use for simple jobs. Unfortunately with fractures as smooth as those occurring in glass they do not make a very solid repair.

Epoxy resin adhesives yellow badly with age. Since glass always fractures cleanly, however, it needs as thin a film of adhesive as possible (the ideal being zero thickness), and in such a thin film any yellowing is correspondingly less noticeable. But gluing with epoxy resin also calls for faultless technique.

WITH CYANOCRYLATES
Accepting, then, that the piece once restored will never be of anything but documentary value, the restorer can set about gluing it together.

78
A glass and crystalware restorer in his workshop.

As with glazed earthenware the first stage is to reassemble the piece in its entirety – sometimes a virtually impossible and in any case highly acrobatic feat – with the aid of transparent adhesive tape. Adhesive is then applied and allowed to infiltrate the fractures. (Glass has an advantage here in that the restorer can see whether the adhesive has penetrated properly.) Any excess adhesive is then softened with paint remover and lifted off with a graver.

If the glass is thick enough, the restorer can glue it more solidly by using a very fine diamond grinding wheel (obtainable from a dental supplier) on a flexible drive arm to grind a barely perceptible path down the centre of the fractured edges occupying

110

about one third of their width. The piece is then reassembled with adhesive tape and the adhesive introduced in the normal way; gaining an extra purchase on the ground path, it will make the repair more solid.

WITH EPOXY RESIN

Gluing with epoxy resin is more solid but very difficult to perform cleanly.

Operating in completely dirt-free conditions, the restorer applies a small quantity of epoxy resin to the fractured edges and reassembles the fragments with the aid of an assistant who sticks adhesive tape on both sides of the glass. When the adhesive is dry the tape is removed and any excess adhesive can be lifted off fairly easily with a graver.

On a piece of opaque pottery no one can see whether there is adhesive all along the fractures. In repairing glass it is important to ensure that there is, otherwise the repair will be unnecessarily obtrusive.

GLUING THICK GLASS

Thick glass (say from the first quarter of this century) is easier to glue, though the restorer should still not expect miracles. Here it is indispensable to rough the centres of the fractured edges with a diamond wheel, and one can risk using a cyanocrylate like an ordinary adhesive, applying it generously to the edges and reassembling the piece fragment by fragment; the fractures are usually so clean that there is little possibility of error.

GLUING A FOOT

An accident that often happens is that for example a Venetian goblet mounted on an elaborately decorated foot demonstrating all the glass-blower's virtuosity becomes separated from the foot at the narrowest point. The restorer is faced with the problem of joining two relatively heavy fragments together with only about half a square centimetre to which he can apply adhesive.

Three solutions are possible.

The first is simply to glue the fragments with cyanocrylate or epoxy resin adhesive after carefully preparing the fractured surfaces with a diamond wheel, choosing one that is like a little circular saw and making several deep, narrow cuts to give the adhesive a really good purchase on both fragments. The repair will still not be a very solid one, but it will hold if the piece is simply going to stand in a glass case in a museum.

The second solution – less elegant but a great deal more solid – consists in boring matching holes of as small a diameter as possible in the middle of the two fractured surfaces. The boring can be done with a diamond bit or with a tiny tube of soft iron turning gently on a little diamond dust. The restorer then glues the fragments together with cyanocrylate adhesive, introducing into the two holes a tiny steel pin that he has filed rough to give it a good purchase on the adhesive. The pin will of course be visible through the glass, but this will not matter too much as long as the job has been done neatly and the restorer has not pushed a gob of yellowing adhesive or a bit of dirt in with it.

The third solution, the most elegant in many cases, is also the most difficult to effect. It is a cross between the Japanese approach and those adaptations of certain Chinese wares by means of a bronze fitting. The restorer joins the two fragments by means of a gold or silver collar, in designing which he may draw his inspiration from the collars used by

Renaissance craftsmen to join together the different components of a rock-crystal goblet.

Assuming the restorer is not a goldsmith as well, he will first take a casting of several centimetres of each of the separated fragments, using an elastomer for the moulds and epoxy resin for the castings. The two epoxy resin stumps are given to a jeweller or goldsmith who can then make the collar without any risk of damaging the piece he is helping to restore. Once the collar has been soundly glued on with white-tinted epoxy resin it should give the impression of having always been there, of having been placed there by the maker of the glass for decorative rather than structural purposes.

Incidentally the third solution is the only one possible when the point of contact has been reduced to nothing by the disappearance of a large chip.

RENEWING MISSING FRAGMENTS

Perfection is of course out of the question when it comes to renewing a missing fragment in a vessel of glass or crystal as thin as a cigarette paper.

If the piece is of outstanding historical and documentary importance it can at a pinch be exhibited incomplete, but if one is set on completing it the following is the best technique.

After gluing together the fragments that are left the restorer turns a block of wood to exactly the profile of the glass, taking his measurements with the aid of callipers. He then selects a sheet of plexiglass of the same thickness as the wall of the glass, softens it (without scorching it) over a red-hot electric resistance heater, wraps it round the turned block, and leaves it to cool. The outline of the missing fragment is carefully traced onto the shaped plexiglass and cut out with a very fine saw. The plexiglass fragment is then glued into place with light applications of cyanocrylate adhesive.

A piece of twentieth-century glass – a Gallé, for example, or a Marinot, or a Navarre – will often call for reconstitution. Here there will be the problem of reproducing the deliberate irregularities – bubbles, colouring, etc. – that the artist introduced into the "metal" for decorative purposes. Such irregularities often turn out to be a help to the restorer, in fact.

This type of reconstitution is done with the most transparent type of polyester available. The restorer makes a wall of modelling clay around the area to be filled. He then applies polyester to the area after adding the appropriate reagents. It is best to apply a generous volume of polyester, despite the extra work involved in carving it down to shape; a larger volume always sets more firmly.

The polyester is ground down with a wheel, then with finer and finer grades of abrasive paper, and finally rottenstoned. Great care must be taken not to scratch the adjacent glass. The repair can be completed by spraying a coat of polyurethane varnish onto the renewed fragment and the area immediately around it, rubbing it down lightly, and giving it a final polish with rottenstone.

Very fine bubbles can be obtained by stirring the polyester with a spatula while it is setting. Larger bubbles can be injected with a hypodermic syringe, though this must be done at exactly the moment when the polyester is beginning to jell; otherwise they will have a tendency to rise.

79
The restorer has completed the neck of an irisated glass in polyester and will now proceed to shape it with the grinding wheel.

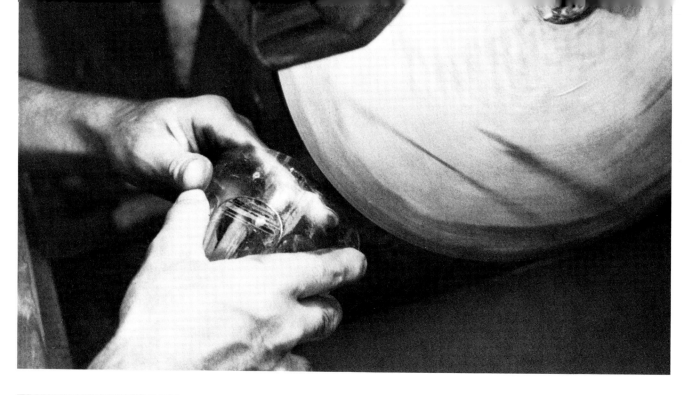

Colouring effects can be achieved with the aid of special colouring agents marketed by the chemical industry. There are all kinds of them available. It is a good idea to ask for samples.

GRINDING DOWN

Nicks and even quite large chips can be treated successfully by grinding. This needs to be done by a specialist. He simply grinds the damaged area down and repolishes it. The shape of the vessel will be altered and the proportions may suffer as a result; still, it is a useful method in some cases.

Needless to say it is out of the question for museographical purposes since it represents an interference with the work of the original glass-maker.

RENEWING MISSING ELEMENTS
WITH PLEXIGLASS

Here I am thinking of those large Renaissance rock-crystal goblets and pitchers decorated with gold, silver gilt, enamel, and precious stones; excellent results have been obtained by carving missing wings, handles, feet, etc. out of a block of plexiglass on the model of a symmetrically matching element or the other piece of a pair. This can be done fairly easily by roughing the block down with a saw, shaping it with a file, and finishing it off with grinding wheel and graver. Polishing is done with a series of little felt burs of different shapes and sizes that, used in conjunction with polishing paste, will reach and polish every nook and cranny of the surface. Such elements could of course be renewed in rock

Glass grinding at Simelio, a Parisian firm specializing in the repair of glass and crystalware.

crystal, but whereas in the nineteenth century there were any number of lapidaries only too delighted to work on this type of piece in, for example, the Naples Collection, nowadays you will be lucky to find anyone who can carve a missing element in rock crystal for an acceptable price.

Antique glass

As far as the restorer is concerned, "antique glass" is not so much glass made before the dawn of the Christian era as glass that has lost its original properties as a result of reacting with the earth in which it lay buried, becoming devitrified and opaque and above all breaking down into wafer-thin flakes as iridescent as a butterfly's wing.

The iridescence so typical of excavated glassware constitutes a large part of its charm and as such ought to be preserved, cleaned, and enhanced by the restorer. It may also help him to achieve a virtually invisible repair.

CLEANING

Sometimes antique glass is found covered with a veritable matrix of totally devitrified material mingled with earth. The object presents an extremely dull appearance, but a flash here and there suggests that the lower layers are magnificently iridescent. The restorer can try removing a film of the outer layer by rubbing it very gently with abrasive paper (he should on no account try to chip it off). Good taste and common sense will dictate how far this process should be taken; for example a

80
The extreme fragility of antique glassware calls for very delicate handling. Here a fragment is set in place with the aid of a stick and a little ball of modelling-clay.

delightful effect can be to have iridescent portions set off by duller areas.

Another way of getting rid of the earth and possibly revealing iridescence underneath is to rinse the piece with water. Particularly stubborn deposits can be removed with local applications of hydrochloric acid.

GLUING

Special problems are involved in gluing antique glass; the procedure is not the same as with modern glass.

For example it is sometimes eggshell thin, which makes it more difficult to reassemble without breaking the fragments further (ill. 80). On the other hand it is not transparent, so that it matters less if the adhesive used to glue it is not transparent, and since it is invariably of archaeological interest the whole problem of invisibility is of secondary importance anyway. Lastly, the use of certain types of adhesive is ruled out by the need to preserve the iridescent effect, which they would remove by penetrating between the flakes. (Iridescence being caused by the refraction of light through the multiple layers of decomposed glass, reintegrating those layers in a mass of adhesive destroys the effect.) Great delicacy is required when handling the fragments during gluing. The iridescent flakes are always extremely fragile and tend to come away on the restorer's sticky fingers, soon leaving the piece devoid of this precious ornament.

Here again the restorer's first choice will be that old stand-by, polyvinyl adhesive, which is very clean to use and disappears without a trace when dry. The thinness of the glass and the fragility of its surface will often make it impossible to use rubber bands or adhesive tape. Gluing is best done in a stream of warm air, and the fragments can be manipulated with the aid of a little ball of modelling clay on the end of a stick.

RENEWING MISSING PORTIONS
OF ANTIQUE GLASS

A fragment missing from the neck of a vase or the foot of a glass can be renewed with polyester, which is allowed to set in position supported by a little cup of adhesive tape or modelling clay. The resultant block is then very carefully shaped with the aid of a little grinding wheel on a flexible drive arm. It is deliberately left unpolished in the interests of museographical honesty; the opaline white of

81
Filling a gap with polyester can be done by first inflating a small rubber balloon inside the piece; this will back the hole and support the polyester while it is setting.

117

unpolished polyester usually harmonizes very well with the overall colour of antique glass.

Filling a hole in the side of a piece of antique glassware is done by first inflating a balloon inside the vessel in such a way as to shutter the missing portion. Polyester is then applied, and the balloon is maintained at the correct pressure until the polyester has set (ill. 81), then it is carefully deflated and removed. The polyester is gently finished with the grinding wheel.

If the restorer wants to go for an invisible repair he can use the store of iridescent flakes he will have carefully saved up from previous jobs on antique glass. These are glued on as they are (pulverizing them would destroy their iridescence). The same procedure can be used to break up the lines of fractures. He can even finish off by applying a little "original" earth mixed with diluted adhesive. This type of restoration is very much open to question, however; it is rarely perfect and smacks of prostitution.

A very fine and highly museographical way of reconstituting a piece of antique glass is to fit panels of unpolished plexiglass in place of the missing fragments and to hold them there by means of lugs glued to the inside of the glass. The polyester fragments can then be given a combed look to distinguish them deliberately from the original glass. This

82
The missing fragment has been reconstituted in the ground colour. The white pattern is being incised. The incision will then be filled with white polyester.

83
The handles are polyester restorations. The illusion is completed by applying irisations that have been salvaged.

is done by finishing the rubbing-down process with a fairly coarse abrasive paper worked always in the same direction. The job will look all the better for it.

STRIPE EFFECTS

The Egyptians used to make small glass vessels in which a number of different "metals" were superimposed or intertwined. Although gluing and even matching the fractured edges of such vessels present no particular problems to the restorer, a certain amount of imagination is needed when it comes to renewing missing portions that carry stripes of different colours.

The best way of setting about this is to reconstitute the entire missing portion with polyester tinted to match the ground colour, and then to polish it (ills. 82 and 83). The restorer then gouges grooves in the renewed portion corresponding to the stripes on the original and fills them with polyester tinted to the appropriate colour or colours. The stripes are then filed down and the whole area polished once more. The result is often perfect.

Generally, since it is virtually impossible to make invisible repairs to glass, the accent will be on elegance and discretion, on precision gluing, on the independence of the renewed elements, and on the neatness of the material used rather than on how closely it imitates the original.

CONCLUSION

And so I come to the end of my attempt to describe and explain the different techniques involved in the restoration of pottery and glass. What I have also tried to show is that, if the hand of man is the finest tool at the restorer's disposal, if its skill and sensitivity, guided and directed by a watchful mind in love with what it is doing, are the principal ingredients of his success, he is getting a lot of help nowadays from the chemical industry in the form of new and better adhesives and plastics.

Granted that here as in medicine, surgery, and *cordon bleu* cookery the individual genius, inventiveness, sureness of touch, and sharpness of vision of the craftsman at work are what counts in the end; these gifts must be backed up not only by a disciplined approach and a solid grasp of technique but also by continually improved materials.

Skill, technique, materials: a magnificient threesome that would make every deceit, every fabrication possible, persuading the restorer that he was some prodigious Mephistopheles endowed with the miraculous power of producing gold coins endlessly from a magic crucible – were it not for the supremacy of professional integrity, which will often place strict limits on what is permissible. Manual dexterity is not the problem; that can be acquired. The problem lies in a sense of what is due and fitting – and in the fact that it is precisely this sense that tends to go by the board as the degree of dexterity increases. The problem is one of self-control, of a firm determination not to err on the side of excess. The problem, in a word, is not to get carried away.

The temptation is terrible to use one's talent to the full. But here, as in other fields, there is usage – and there is "abusage."

TECHNICAL NOTES

GLOSSARY

Body
The part of a piece of pottery that is composed of fired clay, as distinct from the glaze and decoration.

Celadons
A family of early Chinese wares distinguished by its rich gamut of green glazes.

Fitch
A special brush made of polecat hair, useful for applying thin coats of paint or varnish very evenly. It is held at right angles to the surface. Also *to fitch*, to use such a brush.

Glaze
Any vitreous substance applied to the surface of a piece of pottery and fixed by fusion.

Rhython
A type of Greek drinking-vessel fashioned in the shape of an animal.

Saltpetre rot
A white efflorescence found in the body of excavated wares (due to the presence of saltpetre). Advanced saltpetre rot will cause the body to break up into flakes.

Scumbling
The technique of applying a *scumble* or thin coat of paint that is to a greater or lesser degree transparent, allowing the coat underneath to show through accordingly.

Slip
A creamy mixture of finely-ground clay and water used for decorating pottery.

Turning marks
Ridges or grooves left on or in the surface of a piece of pottery by the action of the potter's hands or by a tool as the vessel was turned on the wheel.

WHAT *NOT* TO DO

When cleaning

Allow the fractured edges to rub together
Scrape off old adhesive with a tool
Use harsh cleaning materials on soft wares

When gluing

Overlook an unevenness
File or grind down an ill-fitting fragment
Rub down an unevenness with sandpaper

When filling

Scratch the glaze when rubbing down the fill
Leave the surface of the fill recessed (except for a specific reason)

When retouching

Leave any mistake whatever. You can always remove the paint and start again.

TYPES OF POTTERY

Class	Name and characteristics	Order	Name and characteristics
I	Soft-paste wares (can be cut with a file, argillo-sandy, calciferous, most will melt in a porcelain kiln), twelfth century B.C. to fifteenth century A.D.	1st	Earthenware or terracotta (argillo-sandy body, mat, unglazed surface) Sub-orders: A. figures (cast) B. utensils, bricks, furnaces (cast) C. mat wares, jars, urns (turned)
		2nd	Glazed earthenware (thin silico-alkaline glaze)
		3rd	Glazed earthenware (lead glaze; common faiences)
		4th	Glazed earthenware (tin glaze)
			appendix: tiles, bricks, etc. with vitrified glaze
II	Hard-paste wares (cannot be cut with a file, opaque, argillo-sandy, will not melt), sixteenth to eighteenth centuries.	5th	Fine glazed earthenware (colourless body, vitro-plumbic glaze)
		6th	Stoneware (coloured body, unglazed or with silico-alkaline glaze)
III	Translucent hard-paste wares (argillo-siliceous, alkaline, can be softened), seventeenth to nineteenth centuries	7th	Hard porcelain (kaolin body, feldspathic glaze)
		8th	Natural soft porcelain (argillo-saline, phosphatic, kaolinic body, vitro-plumbic, boracic glaze)
		9th	Artificial soft porcelain (fritted marly-saline body, vitro-plumbic glaze)

EQUIPMENT

General

Daylight from the north, with the window on the restorer's right. Evening light is invariably bad for retouching
Wooden workbenches
A wooden turntable, ball-bearing mounted, to enable the restorer to revolve the object swiftly when retouching or reassembling

For cleaning

A sink with running water
Plastic bowls
Large vessels for boiling
Unlimited supplies of jamjars, etc.
Nailbrushes, nylon and bristle
Large, round, flat-ended brushes
Ordinary brushes with the hairs cropped to half their length to make them stiffer

For gluing

Clamps, spring clips, clothes pins, etc.
Joiners' clamps
Elastic bands, all sizes
Transparent self-adhesive tape
String
Wooden tightening-keys

For filling

Spatulas, all shapes and sizes, made in the workshop out of scrap metal (files, spring leaves, bicycle spokes, etc.) or purchased from a dental supplier
Wooden spatulas
A small plastic bowl
A large glass palette for mixing fill
A glass-marble or porcelain mortar
A drill, with steel and tungsten carbon bits
An electric motor fitted with a rheostat and a flexible drive arm, plus a whole selection of steel and diamond grinding wheels and little felt burs for polishing
Wood rasps
Metal files
A set of rat-tail files
A set of rifflers
A wire brush (for cleaning the files)
A set of pliers, flat-nose, round-nose, and cutting
A fret saw

For retouching

Frosted-glass palettes: slabs of acid-frosted glass 6 mm thick and measuring 24×30 cm (9×12 in.)
A glass muller for grinding pigments
An ivory palette knife (unobtainable commercially; the restorer will have to make his own out of a piano key; the point is that ivory does not stain white pigments)
A palette knife and a painting knife, both steel

Brushes:

Good-quality hog-bristle brushes for retouching large terracottas (also for applying water-based adhesives)

Ordinary brushes with cropped hairs, very useful for flicking on spots of paint (the only way of reproducing certain effects)

Flat sable brushes, all sizes

Pointed polecat-hair or fitch brushes, all sizes

Some agate burnishers
A gold cushion and other leaf-gilding equipment
A miniature spray gun with compressor
A set of china pans

MATERIALS

For cleaning

Dish-washing liquid
Soft soap
Alkali
Detergent (as used for washing down paint)
Hydrochloric acid
Solvents:
Acetone
Xylene
Trichlorethylene
Turpentine
Paint remover
Polyurethane varnish solvents
Alcohol
Benzol

For gluing

Water-based adhesive: polyvinyl acetate
Polymerizable adhesives:
Epoxy resins (slow-setting and fast-setting)
Cyanocrylates

For filling and renewing

Whiting
Very fine modelling plaster
Fast-setting polyester (as used by monumental masons)
A very high-quality polyester (as used for setting insects); should be as transparent as possible; obtainable from artists' materials suppliers
A thixotropic polyester
Epoxy resin, slow and fast-setting (As well as for gluing, these can be used for fillings and castings.)
Epoxy resin putty (useful on some coarse terracottas; not essential)

For casting

Moulds:

A silicone elastomer
A thixotropic silicone elastomer
Modelling clay of a kind that does not disintegrate on contact with elastomer
Dental alginate
Wax (as used by dentists for taking impressions)

Casts:
    Plaster
    Epoxy resin
    Polyester

Metal reinforcement:
    Brass and steel rods in all sizes

For rubbing-down and polishing

Scouring bricks
Cleaning fluid for varnishes and lacquers
Scouring rush
Abrasive paper, all grades (for wet and dry use)
Rottenstone

Varnishes:	*Solvents:*
Clear shellac varnish	Alcohol
French polish	Alcohol
Platinum varnish	Alcohol
Acrylic picture varnish	Turpentine
Restoring varnish	Turpentine
Slow-setting epoxy resin	Trichlorethylene
Rubber varnish	Xylene
Cellulose varnish	Acetone
Polyurethane varnish	Special solvent
Wax varnish	—
Virgin wax	Xylene

BIBLIOGRAPHY

Ceramic Techniques

AUSHER, E. S.: *Technologie de la céramique*, classification des poteries argiles, feldspath, kaolins, quartz, craies, pâtes et couvertes. Outillage céramique, séchage et cuisson. Fours d'essais, décoration des poteries, colorants céramiques. Paris: J.-B. Baillère, 1901.

FOUREST, HENRY PIERRE: *La Céramique*. Saint-Mandé: Editions de la Tourelle, 1948.

SAVAGE, GEORGE: *An Illustrated Dictionary of Ceramics*, defining 3054 terms relating to wares, materials, processes, styles, patterns and shapes from Antiquity to the present day. List of the principal European factories and their marks. London: Thames and Hudson, 1974; New York: Van Nostrand Reinhold, 1974.

Société des Amis du Musée national de Céramique: *Cahiers de la céramique, du verre et des arts du feu*, Sèvres.

Restoration

CROSS, RENA: *China Repairs and Restoration*. London-New York: W. Foulsham and Co., 1972.

EVERARD, BLANCHE: *Traité de peinture à froid sur porcelaine, faïence, biscuit, terre cuite, grès, glace, en supprimant la cuisson*. Paris: Bornemann, 1970.

PLENDERLEITH, H. J.: *La Conservation des antiquités et des œuvres d'art*. Paris: Eyrolles, 1966.

RIS PAQUOT, O. E.: *L'Art de restaurer soi-même les faïences, porcelaines, cristaux, marbres, etc.* Paris: M. Laurens, 1872.

THIAUCOURT, P.: *L'Art de restaurer les faïences et les porcelaines*. Paris: Aubry, 1868.

INDEX

Adhesives, 18, 28, 86, 90. See also specific types of adhesives
Alkali. See Cleaning agents
Ammonia. See Cleaning agents
Angkor, 37
Animal adhesives, 20, 27, 32
Archaeological finds, 10; cleaning of, 23, 24; filling of 53, 63, 72; gluing of, 35, 40, 50

Cambodia, 37
Cellulose, 18, 26
Chalk deposits, 23–26, 51, 99
Chinese wares, 10, 63, 101, 111
Cleaning agents: alkali, 24, 26; ammonia, 24; hydrochloric acid, 23, 24, 26 116. See also Solvents
Colours: for glass, 115, 119. See also Pigments
Corinthian wares, 63
Cretan ware, 65, 88
Cyanocrylates, 28, 49–50, 109, 111

Distortions, 44, 50
Dresden china, 72

Earthenware: See Faience; Glazed earthenware; Soft earthenware; Stoneware; Terracotta
Epoxy resin: cleaning of, 18; filling with, 57, 71 77; with glass, 111; gluing with, 42–44, 50; retouching with, 106–107
Egyptian glass, 119

Faience, 24, 76
Fractures, 13–14; with flaking, 24, 43
Fragments: gluing of, 37–38; renewing of 63, 66, 112

Gallé, 112
Glass: antique, 115–119; modern 109–112
Glaze, 57, 60, 101–103
Glazed earthenware: cleaning of, 14–23; filling of, 54, 56, 66, 76, 77; gluing of 31, 39, 42–44; retouching of, 99, 101
Gluing, 33; degluing 17–18, 20, 23. See also Archaeological finds; Glass; Glazed earthenware; Porcelain; Soft earthenware; Terracotta
Greek pottery: filling of, 54, 56, 72; retouching of, 92
Guimet Museum, 101

Hydrochloric acid. See Cleaning agents

Iraklion, 90
Iridescence, 115, 117, 118

Japanese ware, 71, 101, 108, 111

Kakiemon ware, 71
Khmer restorer, 37
Korean ware, 101

Marinot, 112
Mediums, 86
Metal oxides, 80, 95
Modelling clay, 38, 63
Museographical restoration, 10–11; of glass, 117, 118; gluing for, 28; retouching for, 86, 99

Navarre, 112
Nevers ware, 57, 72

Persian ware, 99
Peruvian wares, 54
Pigments, 54, 80
Plexiglass, 112, 115, 118
Plaster, 39
Plastic, 66
Polyester: filling with, 61, 66, 68, 71; with glass, 112, 118; gluing with, 38–39, 46
Polystyrene, 65
Polyvinyl acetate: for archaeological finds, 32–39; for glass, 117; for glazed earthenware, 42; for retouching of, 99, 101, 102, 107
Porcelain: cleaning of, 14–23; filling of, 54, 60, 71, 76, 77; gluing of, 50; retouching of, 99, 101, 102, 107
Pottery, 8. See also Glazed earthenware; Porcelain; Soft earthenware; Stoneware; Terracotta
Pre-Columbian ware, 31, 38

Renewing elements, 72, 77, 115, 117
Restoration, 9–11. See also Museographical restoration
Retouching, 79; with brush, 103–106; for gloss finish, 99, 101; for mat finish, 85, 86, 90, 85; with spray gun, 106–107

Rhagae. See Persian ware

Saltpetre rot, 26
Scumbling, 85
Shuttering, 63
Silicone elastomer, 76
Solvents: acetone, 18, 26; alcohol, 23–32; paint remover, 20, 40; potassium chloride, 14; trichlorethylene, 44, 106
Soft earthenware: cleaning of, 23; filling of, 53, 54, 65, 72; gluing of, 40
Stoneware, 56, 77, 99
Stucco, 63, 65, 66, 72

Tanagra figurine, 95, 96
Terracotta: filling of, 54; gluing of, 31, 38–39; retouching of, 80, 95, 96
Titanium dioxide. See Whites

Varnish: filling with, 56, 75; gluing with, 32–33; retouching with, 86, 90, 107

Waterproofing, 32–33
Whites, 85–86
Whiting, 54, 86

Photographs by G. Routhier and by the author.

This book was printed by Imprimerie Hertig+Co. S.A., Bienne in March, 1976. Photolithographs by Kreienbühl+Co. S.A., Lucerne. Binding by Burkhardt S.A., Zurich. Layout and production: Yves Buchheim. Editorial: Barbara Perroud-Benson.

Printed in Switzerland

2359